Praise for *Cactus Tracks & Cowboy Philosophy*

"He could make a dead man sit up and laugh!"
—*The Washington Post Book World*

"Baxter Black hog-ties his rhymes with a force emblematic of John Wayne. . . . [He] throws the bull, the cow, the stallion, the mare, common barnyard critters, and even puts the kitchen sink into these pieces with assurance. . . . Just put on yer five-buckle over-shoes, watch where you step, and join the fun."
—*Kirkus Reviews*

"Whether the verses and anecdotes of the 'Cowboy Poet and Former Large Animal Vet' are genuine folk art or a canny and sophisticated simulation, they are genuinely amusing."
—*The Atlantic Monthly*

"Black has a way with words. . . . His prose and poetry are rich in the sights, sounds, smells, tastes, and textures of the ranch, prairie, and high country."
—*Library Journal*

"The short essays and poems collected here. . . . [celebrate] the world of cowboys and farmers, pickup trucks, feed lots, wild horses, baler twine, stock shows, range fires and rodeos."
—*Publishers Weekly*

"Whether you're more at home on the range or sipping cappuccino at Cherry Creek Mall, you will speak in 'Baxterized' rhyming couplets for weeks after finishing the book."
—*Rocky Mountain News*

"If I were asked to name a couple of poets who make a nice living off of their poetry, the names that would come to mind are Yevgeny Yevtushenko and Baxter Black."
—Calvin Trillin

PENGUIN BOOKS

CACTUS TRACKS & COWBOY PHILOSOPHY

Baxter Black is a cowboy poet, cattle feeder, sorry
tame roper, and an irregular commentator on National
Public Radio. He writes a weekly column and makes a
living speaking at agricultural benefits. His first novel,
Hey Cowboy, Wanna Get Lucky? is also available from
Penguin. He lives in Arizona.

Other Books by Baxter Black

A Cowful of Cowboy Poetry
The Cowboy and His Dog
A Rider, A Roper, and a Heck'uva Windmill Man
On the Edge of Common Sense, The Best So Far
Doc, While Yer Here
Coyote Cowboy Poetry
Buckaroo History
Croutons on a Cow Pie
The Buckskin Mare
Cowboy Standard Time
Croutons on a Cow Pie, Volume II
Dunny and the Duck
Hey Cowboy, Wanna Get Lucky?

CACTUS TRACKS

&

COWBOY PHILOSOPHY

Baxter Black

PENGUIN BOOKS

PENGUIN BOOKS
Published by the Penguin Group
Penguin Putnam Inc., 375 Hudson Street,
New York, New York 10014, U.S.A.
Penguin Books Ltd, 27 Wrights Lane,
London W8 5TZ, England
Penguin Books Australia Ltd, Ringwood,
Victoria, Australia
Penguin Books Canada Ltd, 10 Alcorn Avenue,
Toronto, Ontario, Canada M4V 3B2
Penguin Books (N.Z.) Ltd, 182–190 Wairau Road,
Auckland 10, New Zealand
Penguin India, 210 Chiranjiv Tower, 43 Nehru Place,
New Delhi 11009, India

Penguin Books Ltd, Registered Offices:
Harmondsworth, Middlesex, England

First published in the United States of America by Crown Publishers, Inc. 1997
Reprinted by arrangment with Crown Publishers, Inc.
Published in Penguin Books 1998

11 13 15 17 19 20 18 16 14 12

Copyright © Baxter Black, 1997
All rights reserved

THE LIBRARY OF CONGRESS HAS CATALOGUED THE HARDCOVER AS FOLLOWS:
Black, Baxter, 1945–
Cactus tracks & cowboy philosophy / by Baxter Black. —1st ed.
p.   cm.
ISBN 0-609-60122-9 (hc.)
ISBN 0 14 02.7567 3 (pbk.)
1. Veterinarians—West (U.S.)—Literary collections.
2. Cowboys—West (U.S.)—Literary collections.   I. Title.
PS3552.I.288C63   1997
818'.5409—dc21   96–54507

Printed in the United States of America

Except in the United States of America, this book is sold subject to the condition
that it shall not, by way of trade or otherwise, be lent, re-sold, hired out, or otherwise
circulated without the publisher's prior consent in any form of binding or cover other
than that in which it is published and without a similar condition including
this condition being imposed on the subsequent purchaser.

Contents

in chronological order

LIST OF ILLUSTRATIONS ix
INTRODUCTION 1
HANGIN' ON, HOPIN' AND PRAYIN' FOR RAIN 3
RALPH'S TREE 5
ALL I WANT FOR CHRISTMAS 8
RUNNIN' WILD HORSES 10
ANONYMOUS END 13
HOME THE HARD WAY 15
A LESSON IN LIFE 17
THE SALES CALL 19
A LOVE STORY 21
HOLIDAY TRAVELERS 23
THE CAR WASH 25
THE PRACTITIONER'S LOT 27
AARP! 29
RANGE FIRE 32
CHAUVINIST? WHO ME? 35
WOMEN! 37
TOLERANCE 39
CAUGHT IN THE ACT 41
RUDOLPH'S NIGHT OFF 44
GRANDMA'S PICTURE BOX 47
SHEEPMEN, BORDER COLLIES, AND MULES 49
THE CONSULTANT 51
DEER RASSLIN' 53

Contents

JUST FRIENDS 55

TRIGGERNOMETRY 57

ONEUPSMANSHIP 59

THE ROPIN' VET 61

THE HERD SIRE 63

THE COWBOY'S GUIDE TO VEGETARIANS 66

A VEGETARIAN'S GUIDE TO COWBOYS 68

THE STOCK DOG DEMONSTRATION 70

COWBOY PRESERVES 72

FEAR OF FLYING 74

JANUARY, FEBRUARY, MUD 76

BOLLER'S COMMENTS 78

ANOTHER GOOD MAN GONE 79

LOST 81

ARDEL'S BULL 83

DOG EMOTIONS 85

3% MARKUP 88

SECRET SEASONING 90

FEAST OR FAMINE 92

LOOSE COW 94

THRIFTY 96

GARTHED OUT! 98

PART INDIAN 100

WHITE OAKS RODEO 102

JOE AND MARIA 104

MY KINDA TRUCK 108

VERN'S WRECK 110

THE COWBOY AND HIS TAPEWORM 112

BENTLEY THE BORN-AGAIN BULL 114

BUFFALO TRACKS 116

THE GREAT CHICKEN RUN 118

DISAPPEARING DIGITS 120

LOOKIN' BACK 122

CONTENTS

POLITICAL CORRECTNESS 124

THE BIG HIGH AND LONESOME 126

LANDSCAPING 128

IT AIN'T EASY BEIN' A COWBOY 131

THE OLD STOVE-UP COWBOYS OF AMERICA 133

THE GRAPEVINE 135

THE TRANQUILIZER GUN 137

KEEPIN' BUSY 139

THE EPITAPH 141

A FOX IN THE HENHOUSE 143

PARAKEETS AND DOGS 145

COWBOY TIME 147

THE FLOOD 149

BALIN' WHEAT 151

THE STARR VALLEY BEAN FIELD WAR 153

CHICAGO'S BRATWURST 155

THE NATIONAL INSECT 157

MOOSE ALERT 160

WHAT'S CHRISTMAS TO A COW? 162

COLD FEET 164

PIG TALES 166

TOMBSTONE OF CANAAN 169

NEAT AND TIDY CALVING 171

THE C-SECTION 173

THE WILDERNESS WALL 175

ADVICE COLUMN 177

BORDER COLLIES 179

HE SANG "LITTLE JOE THE WRANGLER" 181

THE OUTBACK 186

TRUTH IN LABELING 188

IT'S THE LAW 191

THE FIRST COWBOY THANKSGIVING 193

THE REINDEER FLU 195

CONTENTS

COWBOY MENTALITY 197

THE VALDEZ 199

THE MOUNTAIN 201

OF PIGS AND POULTRY 203

COW XTRACTOR 205

THE HUNTER'S SON 207

DOGGONE COUNTRY 209

THE ROMANTIC COWBOY 211

A COWBOY PARADE 213

COW ATTACK 216

ANTI-SMOKIN' DEVICE 218

HIGH COST OF RECYCLING 220

IN THE DOGHOUSE 222

INHERITING THE FAMILY FARM 224

THE LOST CHICKEN 226

WORKIN' FOR WAGES 228

MINNESOTA OREOS 230

OREOS APOLOGY 232

LEROY AND TOM 234

COWBOY VEGETARIAN COOKBOOK 236

NOAH'S DISPERSAL SALE 238

DUCT TAPE IN AGRICULTURE 240

COW POLYGAMY 243

SHOEIN' PIGEYE 245

NATURE FILMS 247

THE HOULIHAN 249

BABE 251

RELIGIOUS REFLECTIONS 254

JUST WORDS 256

HERE COME DE JUDGE 258

GLOSSARY 261

NPR AIR DATES 267

Illustrations

1. Ralph's Tree. By Dave Holl.

2. Caught in the Act. By Charlie Marsh.

3. The Herd Sire. By Don Gill.

4. Dog Emotions. By Bob Black.

5. Joe and Maria. By Dave Holl.

6. Landscaping. By Charlie Marsh.

7. The Old Stove-Up Cowboys of America. By Ace Reid.

8. National Insect. By Don Gill.

9. Pig Tales. By Bob Black.

10. Truth in Labeling. By Charlie Marsh.

11. Cowboy Parade. By Dave Holl.

12. Duct Tape. By Don Gill.

13. Babe. By Bob Black.

Introduction

CONFESSIONS OF A
FORMER LARGE ANIMAL VETERINARIAN

Did you ever look around in your life and say, *"How did I get here? And furthermore, where am I?"*

I've always liked Stephen Wright's observation that goes, *"Ya know when you lean back in a chair till it's just about to tip over and you teeter on the brink? I feel like that all the time."*

I make a living as a poet. And it's a good living . . . though a little hard to get a loan. I do speeches at agricultural banquets and sell my books of cowboy poetry. I have been doing it since the fall of 1982, when the agribusiness company I was working for changed hands. They looked around and said, *"Bax, we need to get rid of some dead wood and yer the only thing floating."*

So while I was preparing my résumé to go to work for another feedlot or ranch outfit, I accepted a few calls inviting me to speak at the corn growers or cattlefeeders annual banquet. And, in a nutshell (or cod, in my business), the phone has never quit ringing. My résumé still sits in the pile of things to finish.

I have always wanted to be in the cow business. I studied animal husbandry at New Mexico State University and completed a veterinary degree at Colorado State University in 1969, then began a career as a company vet for large livestock operations. I have worked and lived in the mountain West tending critters and being a part of the lifestyle I love.

I have been a fan and listener of National Public Radio for many years. In 1988, Yellowstone Park caught on fire. The West was in the grip of a drought. I had written some poems about "hot and

1

dry" and sent one to NPR. They called back and asked if they could run it on the air. I was flattered. I said, *"Of course!"* And they made the fateful error of asking, *"Do you have anything else?"*

Since then I have continued to send them poems and stories. They have been kind enough to run many of them. This book is a complete compilation of those commentaries that NPR's *Morning Edition* has aired from 1988 through the deadline for publication of this book.

These commentaries are about the world I live in: cowboys, animals, farmers, life outside the city limits, modern agriculture, and ancient traditions. They are mostly funny because of that close relationship between humor and tragedy. My world is one in which people have a lot of wrecks. Cow wrecks; horse wrecks; financial wrecks; flood, fire, and drought wrecks. Laughing at our "wrecks" seems to make the tribulations of our lifestyle easier to handle.

For instance, if yer in the corral and one of yer friends gets bucked off, everybody runs over there real quick to make sure he's all right. If he's alive, ya start tellin' the story right away. If he's dead . . . you wait a couple days.

I appreciate and value my association with NPR and my acceptance by its listeners, who are mostly from outside my world. As to why I am included, I can only quote one of the producers who, when I asked him why I was on *Morning Edition,* replied, "Because you're the only one we know from *out there.*"

It gives me great pleasure to dedicate this collection of commentaries to the people who work at National Public Radio—good people, with a sense of duty, fairness, and modesty, who serve a calling as well as a deadline or a paycheck.

I am honored to be a part.

Ah, friends . . . this was my first. In July 1988, I recorded this poem in my small studio and mailed it in. An arrow in the sky. Columbus licking his finger and holding it in the wind. St. Peter taking his first step off the boat. Dukakis finally saying, "What the heck, what have I got to lose?"

If I had known the depth of obsession for quality, authenticity, and integrity striven for by NPR, I might have been too intimidated to fly my flag in front of their scrutiny. But blissful ignorance carried the day.

HANGIN' ON, HOPIN' AND
PRAYIN' FOR RAIN

There's a fingernail moon hangin' low in the sky.
The crickets make small talk as he passes by.

As the gentlest breeze stirs what's left of his hair
He spits and he sniffs it, but no moisture there.

He stares at the field and remembers the year
These same eighty acres paid the loan free and clear.

But these last thirty days have scared him to death.
The dirt's as dry as a horny toad's breath.

He called up his banker after supper tonight
They talked for an hour and he's sure gettin' tight.

Ol' Thelma had kissed him and went on to bed
So he took a walk, thought it might clear his head.

The doctor has told him he has to slow down,
Sell out the home place and move into town.

"Move into town! What the hell would he do?"
He shook off the thought and took a fresh chew.

A bachelor cloud, thin as fog on a mirror,
Crossed over the moon and then disappeared.

He sniffs at the air that's still dry as a bone,
And takes one more look at the seeds that he's sown.

He'll be back tomorrow if somethin' don't change,
Just hangin' on, hopin' and prayin' for rain.

By the end of the summer of 1988, Yellowstone Park was still casting a smoky pall over the western plains. They, too, were dry and flammable. I read about this man from Bainville, Montana, and called him. He was staying with his daughter in Williston, North Dakota, when we talked. He sounded tired.

RALPH'S TREE

Ralph planted the tree next to the house so it would get runoff from the roof. He put it outside the bathroom window so he and Mary could see it often. As the years slid by Ralph gave it special care. It was strange to see a grizzled old rancher fondly tending his tree. But it grew, which was no small accomplishment in the sun-baked prairie of eastern Montana. It withstood the blizzards and dry spells, the searing wind and meager soil, just like the people who inhabit that hard country.

The tree didn't exactly flourish but it lived and grew. It was a symbol. It marked a spot of civilization in an unforgiving land. Ralph rested easier knowing the tree grew in his yard. It gave Mary comfort.

Birds came and nested in it. It stood as tall as it could and did its best to repay Ralph's attention by shading a little more of the house every year. Although Ralph would probably never say it, I figger he loved that tree.

I can understand. I've spent my life planting trees. Wherever I've lived trees were not plentiful . . . the panhandle of Texas, southern New Mexico, the California desert, the sagebrush country of Idaho, and the plains of Colorado. I'd move into a place and plant a few trees. I had to lay pretty flat to get any shade. Then I'd move on before I could hang a hammock. Yup, I know how Ralph felt about his tree.

The Empire Builder, Amtrak's pride of the north, runs from

Chicago to Spokane. It comes through Ralph's country. Eastern Montana was dry as a Death Valley dirt road that summer of '88. Sparks from the train started a range fire. The wall of flame was thirty feet high and moving at forty miles per hour when Ralph smelled the smoke. He and Mary escaped with their lives and little else. The house, the outbuildings, the machinery, and the garden were burned to the ground. They'd been on the ranch fifty-eight years. *Fifty-eight years.*

They're staying in town now. Their lawyer is working on a settlement with the railroad. It'll take time. Something Ralph doesn't want to waste. He's eighty-one.

Ralph's tree is a stick. As dead as a steel post. As dead as a dream.

Ralph, my heart goes out to you, sir. But I know as sure as the sun comes up tomorrow, you have to plant another tree . . . and soon.

Then this winter you can look forward to spring, when that little tree will leaf out and start casting a shadow on the ashes of your pain.

There have been times in my life when I was "down to no keys." Toilet paper neatly folded and placed inside your hatband will make it fit tighter, and newspaper wadded underneath your shirt is good insulation. I did this poem later on Johnny Carson's show. He was particularly empathetic.

ALL I WANT FOR CHRISTMAS

All my clothes are laundry
    All my socks are full'a holes
I've got t.p. in my hatband
    And cardboard in my soles.

    I've stuffed the want ad section
        Underneath my long-john shirt
    And my jacket's held together
        By dehornin' blood and dirt.

The leather on my bridle's
    Been fixed so many times
My horse looks like that fence post
    Where we hang the baler twine.

    When I bought that horse he was
        As good as most around
    But when I sold 'im last month
        He brought thirteen cents a pound.

I've been unable lately
    To invest in purebred cows
Since my ex-wives and their lawyers
    Are dependents of mine now.

See, my first wife took my saddle
The second skinned my hide
The third one got my deer head
And the last one took my pride.

I've had a run of bad luck
But I think it's gonna peak
'Cause my dog that used to bite me
Got run over just last week.

So all I want for Christmas
Is whatever you can leave
But I'd settle for a new wife
Who would stay through New Year's Eve.

*When I went to work for a big cow outfit in the Northwest in 1970
they were still runnin' wild horses. It was majestic. But I wondered,
what with all the griping I heard from the livestock operators, why so
many wild horses still existed. I soon learned that most of the ranchers tried to keep a decent stallion with the bands. Their goal, it
seemed, was not extermination but keeping numbers manageable
and the quality improving.*

*But I also observed that those who enjoyed the chase the most were
the cowboys. Men who had no vested interest in either the horses or
the land. It struck me that they felt a bond with the beasts racing
ahead of them.*

Runnin' Wild Horses

*The chase, the chase, the race is on
The mustangs in the lead
The cowboys hot behind the band
Like centaurs, blurred with speed*

*The horses' necks are wringin' wet
From keepin' up the pace
And tears cut tracks into the dust
Upon the rider's face*

*The rank ol' mare sniffs out the trail
While never breakin' stride
But fast behind the wranglers come
Relentless, on they ride*

*Until the canyon walls close in
And punch 'em through the gap
Where bottled up, they paw and watch
The cowboy shut the trap*

And that's the way it's been out west
Since Cortez turned 'em loose
We thinned the dinks and with the herd
We kept an easy truce

But someone said they'd all die off
If cowboys had their way
So they outlawed runnin' horses
But who am I to say

'Cause, hell, I'm gettin' older, boys
And though I miss the chase
His time, like mine, has come and gone
We're both so out of place

The glamour of our way of life
Belies our common fate
I'm livin' off my pension check
And he's a ward of state

But what a time. When he and I
Ran hard across the land
Me breathin' heavy down his neck
Him wearin' no man's brand

No papers gave us ownership
To all the ground we trod
But it belonged to me and him
As sure as there's a God

And if I could, I'd wish for him
And for myself, likewise
To finally cross the Great Divide
Away from pryin' eyes

So in the end he has a chance
To die with dignity
His carcass laid to rest out there
Where livin', he ran free

And coyotes chew his moldered bones
A fitting epilogue
Instead of smashed up in a can
For someone's townhouse dog.

ANONYMOUS END

I'm here at an old pal's funeral.
    Not too many people have come.
    Just a few of us boys from the outfit
So he don't go out like a bum.

    Seems like I've known him forever
        As I look back over the years.
        We've rode several wagons together
    And shared a couple of beers.

He never quite made it to foreman
    But then, of course, neither have I.
    He always sorta stayed to the center
Just kind of a regular guy.

    He'd always chip in for a party
        Though he was never one to get loud.
        Everything that he did was just average.
    He never stood out in a crowd.

He was fair with a rope and a rifle,
    He was never early or late,
    In the pickup he rode in the middle
So he'd never open a gate.

    Conversin' with him was plum easy.
        He never had too much to say,
        No matter what question you'd ask him
    The answer was always, "Okay."

Well, they've lowered him down to the hardpan
　　And we've sung "Shall we gather at."
　　　　They've asked for a moment of silence
And everyone's holdin' their hat.

　　Now the preacher is askin' me kindly
　　　　To say a few words at his death
　　　　　　So I mumble, and say, "He was steady."
　　Then I pause and take a deep breath,

But I'm too choked up to continue.
　　The crowd thinks I've been overcame
　　　　But the mason has screwed up his tombstone
And I can't remember his name!

As you will oft hear repeated in my notes, this was told to me as a true story. 'Course, by the time it filters through my metaphors, petit fours, and two-by-fours, one might say it's been fictionalized—or, as we say at my house, Baxterized.

HOME THE HARD WAY

They'd been out visiting friends in Wyoming for a week. Jesse'd had a good time but he was itchy to get back to the ranch near Lemmon, South Dakota. They pulled out Friday morning before daylight. Jesse drove . . . in self-defense. His darlin' wife, for all her virtues, possessed an unerring sense of misdirection. North, to her, was a lisping Viking. West was what Elmer Fudd did when he was tired. She had trouble with the concept of distances. She'd heard of Miles Hare, Miles Standish, and Miles Davis, but she couldn't relate them to highway signs. She thought the odometer was aptly named.

By midafternoon Jesse was wore out. After cautiously checking the map he decided there was no way to get lost the rest of the way home, so, reluctantly, he asked his wife to drive. He walked back to the little travel trailer they were pulling, threw her an encouraging wave, and climbed in.

As she picked up speed Jesse peeled down to his shorts and lay on the bed. He was dreamin' of downed wire and water gaps when something woke him. They were stopped? He slid over to the door, stepped out on the shoulder, and walked around the end of the trailer. He took a peek and realized they were at a stop sign at a sleepy little crossroads.

"At least we're not lost," he thought gratefully. Then he heard the crunch of gravel! In a desperate lunge he almost caught the aluminum awning strut, but he stepped on a bottle cap and skittered sideways like a bad billiards shot!

He shouted and ran after her, mincing down the highway in a sort of plucked chicken ballet. She drove merrily off.

He stood alongside the road, sore-footed, white, embarrassed, and hatless in his threadbare, holey Fruit of the Looms with the frayed elastic and baggy seat. He looked like Cupid gone to seed.

Jesse tiptoed over to the little collection of dilapidated buildings and borrowed a pair of old coveralls from a suspicious tradesman. He finally convinced this local that he was not an escaped lunatic and begged a ride home.

He didn't figger he could catch his wife, so he directed this Good Samaritan to a shortcut. Jesse beat his wife home, tipped the wary driver, and went out to water the lawn.

She came whippin' up the driveway, saw him setting the sprinkler on the dry spot, and drove plum through the garage . . . without activating the automatic garage door opener, then derailed near the propane tank in the backyard!

It was a story that wasn't near as funny the first time he explained it to the insurance adjuster.

"Bein' a dad ain't easy. . . ."

A LESSON IN LIFE

Since the dawning of time one generation has been passing on knowledge and experience to the following generation. From mother pterodactyls pushing their babies out of the nest to secret tribal rituals of manhood, it has continued through the ages.

This teaching is no small responsibility. The continuation of life on earth depends upon it, thus each parent must try.

My daughter started a 4-H rabbit project. She purchased three head.

"How much?" I asked, remembering my rabbit days thirty years before.

"Twelve dollars each."

"Twelve dollars!" I ranted and raved, partly for show. I was conscious that a lesson in life was to be learned. Wisdom to be passed. I explained the necessity to bargain, to dicker, to trade! I felt like a mother leopard stalking and slaying some crippled gnu in front of her clumsy, big-footed cubs!

Two weeks later I was in Wisner, Nebraska, visiting with Del and Karen. They wanted to buy my books and mentioned they were in the rabbit business. A light flickered between my ears! I realized this was the perfect opportunity for me to display a shining example of bartering to my daughter.

Yes, they were willing to trade a nice doe for the books. And yes, they would even put her in with the buck that night.

I picked up the newly bred doe the next morning and headed to the Omaha airport.

When I got to the counter, the ticket agent asked if I had anything to check. I told her no, only carry-ons.

"What's that in the box?" she asked.

"Rabbit."

"Is he going with you?"

"Yup. But don't worry, no special meals are required, ha, ha . . . I'll just slide her under the seat."

"I'm sorry, sir, there is a fee for shipping pets . . . thirty dollars . . . your plane is leaving in fifteen minutes."

With a sour look I gave her my credit card. *Zip.*

"What will you be shipping it in?"

"This box," I bluffed. "It's taped up good and has airholes."

"I'm sorry, sir. That's not an officially approved airline pet container."

"Great!" I fumed. "Where am I supposed to get an officially approved airline pet container? The plane leaves in ten minutes!"

"We have them for sale . . . thirty-five dollars . . ." *Zip.*

Well, I got home with the doe. I managed to turn my fiasco into a good lesson in livestock economics (by leaving out a few details). My daughter was impressed.

We waited expectantly for the thirty-two-day gestation period to end and for the doe to have baby bunnies. Then I'd rise to Father First Class. It came, she didn't, and I'm still trying. *Zip.*

Hilda is a rancher in Wyoming. Her story is a typical rubbing of cultural tectonic plates.

THE SALES CALL

A ranch woman has a lot in common with a prisoner in solitary confinement. She is often starved for conversation. This isn't meant to be a reflection on her husband, if she has one, 'cause he spends all day talkin' to the dog, his horse, stray cows, passing motorists, and itinerant mammals, and it kinda depletes his normally plentiful wit. By the time he comes in for supper all he can do is grunt and fall asleep in the Barcalounger.

So when a stranger shows up at the ranch, he's usually welcome company. Which is why there is a grain of truth in the old joke that begins, "Did you hear the one about the farmer's wife and the traveling salesman?"

Hilda found herself visiting at Molly's ranch home one afternoon. It was a visit that had to be planned since Molly lived forty miles from town. Just as they were pouring the second cup, they heard a knock on the door. Molly answered. She was nearly bowled over by a frayed-looking man pulling a vacuum cleaner behind him like a gut-shot varmint draggin' his entrails!

He spoke with the conviction of an evangelist down to his last parishioner.

Molly started to say something but he raised a hand in protest. *"Afternoon, ladies, dee-lighted to catch all of you home! Was just passin' through and saw your cars in the drive. Beautiful home—by the way, I see you collect antique kerosene lanterns. . . . This is your lucky day . . . both of you!*

"I happen to represent Takum and Run, Chicago, Illinois, manufacturers of the finest vacuum cleaners in the free world today! The

*Suckitup Two with power nozzle and self-cleaning dander attach-
ment . . . nice woodstove, there . . . for hard-to-pet dogs . . ."*

He talked without letup for forty-five minutes while the ladies
sat amazed at his stamina. They drew back in astonishment when
he upended a plastic feed sack on Molly's shag carpet! Steel balls,
charcoal briquets, chicken bones, sawdust, fingernail clippings,
volcanic ash, and soybean meal cascaded into a pile!

He spread it across the carpet with a sweep of his hand. *"And to
prove everything I said is the gospel truth, if this vacuum cleaner
doesn't pick up every speck of this mess I've made, I'll get down on my
hands and knees and lick it up myself!"*

Molly leaned forward. "You better git out yer Chapstick, Sonny.
I ain't got no 'lectricity!"

Sometimes when I consider doin' a commentary about a true instance, I have to weigh the impact it might have on the people involved. The family in this story and their community are not the kind to air their emotions in public. I have seen the man and the youngest son in the years since. They have gone on with their lives. I stuck to the true story but I left out the name of the town to protect their privacy.

A LOVE STORY

This is a love story.

In a small ranching community in the West there lived a man, his wife, and their four children. They were no different from their neighbors. They ran cows, built fence, and did their part to keep their little town alive.

The children attended the local school. Students numbered less than a hundred. But the remoteness of the area instilled a strong interdependence among the ranchers, families, and townies.

The man and his wife lived in his folks' old house on the ranch. They planned to remodel someday but the vagaries of the cattle business, the demand for routine ranch improvements, and the appetite of four teenagers combined to prevent any real home improvements.

When the youngest son began high school, the man dared to dream of the future. One where his wife could quit her town job and he could spend more time with her. For even after twenty years he never tired of her company.

Cancer, the assassin, drew down and shot out the light of his life.

His grief was deep. The community put their arms around this proud man and his family. They did what neighbors do. As the months passed, they were always there. Watching after his children while loneliness ground away at his broken heart. They watched over him, as well.

The fall that his youngest began his senior year the man sold his cow herd. The market was good and his interest in the ranch had waned.

One day I got a phone call from him. He introduced himself and invited me to speak at his son's graduation. I didn't recognize the name of the town. He said there were six in the graduating class.

Arrangements were made. He sponsored a big barbecue that afternoon. Four hundred attended. He took a few moments before my introduction at commencement that evening to address the crowd. I was unaware of his tragedy. He spoke simply but expressed his appreciation to his friends and neighbors. He never mentioned his loss. It was unnecessary. In a community like this, everyone knew.

Afterward some of us gathered in his living room for a nightcap. A few friends, his four kids, he, and I. It was comfortable. The new graduate opened his gifts and spoke of his plans with the conviction and anxiety of youth. Nobody asked the man about his plans, but you could hear the page turning in his life.

I guess the hand-lettered sign hangin' on his gatepost out by the road said it all.

YAHOO! THE LAST ONE FINALLY GRADUATED!

THANKS FRIENDS. **RANCH FOR SALE**

I was single for several years and developed friendships with several other single nondomesticated cowboy types like myself. Ducks of a feather hang out like old bulls in the summer or adolescent baboons on jungle street corners. After I married, I continued the friendships. Now, these are not the kind of people you would normally have in your home. So they were always available on Thanksgiving. For a few years my wife and I had them all for Thanksgiving week.

This tale is just part of the ongoing saga.

HOLIDAY TRAVELERS

There is nothing more enjoyable than having friends come in for the holidays. We had a bunch coming from Texas, Nebraska, Wyoming, Oklahoma, Colorado, and points west. Everyone was in and accounted for by ten P.M. the night before, everyone save our wayward wrangler, Pinto.

We knew he had left Idaho on the Gelded Zephyr, Amtrak's answer to Braniff Airways. He was several hours overdue, but we had not yet begun to worry. See, cowboys are often inattentive to instructions, inefficient in their methods of travel, and seldom ruled by schedules, but they possess a dogged narrow-mindedness when in pursuit of a good time.

We all sacked out. The phone rang at three A.M.

"Hi, Bax. . . . Did I git you up?"

"Pinto! Where are you?"

"At a rest area between Rawlins and Green River."

My foggy mind tried to place his train two hundred miles off course at a rest area in Wyoming. "Are you all right?"

"Yeah. Thank goodness we didn't hit the building."

This horrific tale began uneventfully with Pinto arriving in Salt Lake City from Boise four hours late. He was awakened by an eight-to-fiver who ordered him to disembark. He was herded into the depot with his fellow travelers, who were told their connecting train had left without them. They were to board a bus that would carry them to Denver.

Pinto approached the ticket window to register his complaint. The discussion was spirited. The crowd cheered him on.

The police weren't called until Pinto reached through the little ticket window to straighten the clerk's tie and accidentally pulled him up against the glass, flattening his nose.

Quickly departing the depot, he called his friend in Salt Lake City (we'll call him Joe), who agreed to drive him to Denver. Fourteen hours and 190 miles down the road, Pinto was asleep on the passenger side.

When he woke up, the car was coming out of the bar ditch doing sixty-five miles per hour! It didn't begin spinning till the semi (going their way, fortunately) hit them a glancing blow and the car careened off the other side like *Voyager* rounding Jupiter and accelerating toward Uranus.

Pinto and Joe came to a sudden stop at a cement-and-steel picnic table. Joe went back with the Sweetwater County Sheriff. Pinto was phoning me from the rest area.

"So don't worry, Bax, I'll hitch a ride to Cheyenne. Maybe you can pick me up there."

"Fine," I said. Then I heard him speaking to someone.

"The ladies' is on the right. . . . Are you going east?"

I knew nothing could stop him now.

THE CAR WASH

I'm on my ninth pickup. Most of 'em have been Fords. No reason in particular. I wasn't rodeo hand enough to have a Dodge, farmer enough to drive an IH, or rich enough to own a Jimmy. I usually buy secondhand vehicles. It's important that they be mechanically simple. I always thought it was a good sign when I could open the hood and see the road beneath the engine.

I've got a Ford and a Chevy now. Both of 'em '69s. It's a lot easier to work on the Ford, which is a great advantage. The Chevy's a little more crowded under the hood, but I never have to work on it anyhow, it just keeps runnin'.

So I don't know which is the better truck.

My pickup's no different from the average farm truck. The driver's-side cushion is wore through, one window roller is a Vise-Grip. There are four gloves on the seat; none of 'em match. The jockey box is full of blinker lights, Phillips screws, electrical connections, needles, old syringes, valuable papers, and extra keys to who knows what. Under the seat is a chain, a tree saw, a bird's nest, an official issue tire iron (unused), ant poison, a lumber store red flag, and a University of Wyoming archaeological dig.

I never wash it. Lane learned that lesson the hard way. He pulled into the automatic car wash. Loretta took the dog and waited while Lane rode it through.

He sat there enjoyin' a moment's peace and marveled at the modern technology. He watched the soaper, then the big whirling brushes spin up the hood, climb the windshield, and crawl over the cab. He remarked to himself how powerfully efficient, safe, and virtually foolproof the machinery was. "Amazin'," he smiled to himself. That was about the time the whirling dervish dropped into the bed of his pickup!

It sounded like a chain saw rippin' through a fifty-five-gallon drum. Buckets, paint cans, and an airplane wheel sailed out into the street like depth charges! Horseshoes, old bolts, pieces of a disassembled lawn mower carburetor, nails, and a socket set shot through the air like machine-gun fire!

The big brush squealed in pain as a steel fence post went through the observation window! The unit shorted out before the attendant called 911.

Lane spent four hours peelin' three hundred yards of baler twine, twelve feet of hog wire, a log chain, two halters, and a thirty-five-foot nylon rope out of the equipment. By the time he got to sweepin' up, most of the co-op dog food had dissolved and he could hose it out with the leaves and a half a bale of alfalfa.

Now when he goes to the car wash, he leaves his dog in the back of the pickup. Sort of an early warning device.

On closer examination it occurs to me that lots of my stories and poems have "biological" content. I guess you could look up calculi and prolapse.

THE PRACTITIONER'S LOT

Today in the world of modern vets
I've lost my place in line.
My colleagues have prospered as specialists
In therio or swine.

I see their achievements in magazines,
Their articles in print.
They've developed a cure for seedy warts
With after-dinner mints,

Or they're recognized as the final word
In matters so complex
That I can't pronounce what they're working on
Much less, what it affects!

I spend my days at the back of a cow
Usually up to my chin
In the process of pullin' somethin' out
Or pushin' it back in!

Or I'm tryin' to pass a catheter
To move a calculi
While the cat is tearin' my arm to shreds
And sprayin' my good tie!

I dream to discover a new technique
But it's not meant to be.
The chances are slim that they'd even name
A prolapse after me!

But I'm thankful I've got a good practice
With loyal clientele
Who, in spite of my vast shortcomings, still
Try and speak of me well.

Why, just last week two farmers were talkin'
Outside my clinic door.
"Doc ain't perfect, but for our little town
We couldn't ask for more."

"Yeah, I'll agree," the second one answered,
"I've given it some thought,
With Doc you always git yer money's worth
But . . . he don't charge a lot!"

This was one of the most popular poems ever to run on my NPR com-
mentaries, according to listener response. As you might imagine,
NPR does not run everything I send them. I try not to question their
judgment. When I submitted this piece they chose not to air it. Sev-
eral weeks went by. So I called my producer and suggested that it was
certainly a popular poem and would he reconsider. He said, "But it's
such a controversial issue." I said, "This is public radio."

AARP!

Of late there's been a modest debate
involving the wearing of fur.
There's some even swears anybody who wears it
is flawed in their character.

Yet others will fight to maintain their right
to wear what they dang well please
But the answer lies in a compromise
that sets both minds at ease.

Imagine two friends at opposite ends
who meet and do lunch once a week.
Their friendship is tried when they gather outside
a Beverly Hills boutique.

"Sylvia, oh my soul, is that a mink stole?
Please tell me it's fake from Goodwill!"
"Yes, Babs, it is mink, but it's not what you think,
because . . . it's designer roadkill!"

Oh, sure, you scoff, but don't blow it off
it's the wisdom of Solomon's voice.
The perfect solution, it grants absolution
yet leaves the owner Pro Choice.

Wisdom so pure should forever endure
and percolate into your soul
So I'm the head jack of the Animal Accident Recovery Patrol!

The AARP!, which is Harry and me,
are on the road every night
To gently remind you that mess left behind you
is more than a buzzard's delight.

Carry your trowel for mammal or fowl
to collect your vehicular blooper.
In time you will find yucky's all in your mind,
no worse than a pooper scooper.

Plus, you'll be amazed how activists praise you
for doin' what you think is right
And no trapper'd object if you stopped to collect
things that go bump in the night.

But treat it with care, waste not a hare,
be sorry, but don't sit and pine,
'Cause accidents happen when yer both overlappin'
the double yellow line.

So salvage your plunder and render your blunder
into a warm winter coat
And remember our motto as you know you otto
it follows, and herein I quote:

"MAKE IT A HABIT TO PICK UP YOUR RABBIT.
DON'T LEAVE HIM TO DRY IN THE SUN.
FOR THE SAKE OF A GARMENT, RECYCLE YOUR VARMINT,
IT'S TACKY TO JUST HIT AND RUN!"

This poem engendered a big response from listeners. I have seen several big range fires in my life. They are frightening. One summer night in the early '70s, I was driving east on I-85 from Boise. To the north, in the direction of Smith's Ferry, I could see lightning against the silhouetted Sawtooth Mountains. I wrote down the first line of this poem. At the time I was not a poet. But years later I watched the big range fires that followed that terrible summer Yellowstone burned.

The first line came back and, as they say, the poem wrote itself.

RANGE FIRE

Lightning cracked across the sky like veins on the back of your hand.
  It reached a fiery finger out as if in reprimand
  And torched a crippled cottonwood that leaned against the sky
While grass and sagebrush hunkered down that hellish hot July.

  The cottonwood exploded! And shot its flaming seeds
    Like comets into kerosene, igniting all the weeds.
    The air was thick as dog's breath when the fire's feet hit the
      ground.
  It licked its pyrogenic lips and then it looked around.

The prairie lay defenseless in the pathway of the beast.
  It seemed to search the further hills and pointed to the east,
  Then charged! Like some blind arsonist, some heathen hell on
    wheels
With its felonous companion, the wind, hot on his heels.

  The varmints ran like lemmings in the shadow of the flame
    While high above a red-tailed hawk flew circles, taking aim.
    He spied a frazzled prairie dog and banked into a dive
  But the stoker saw him comin' and fried 'em both alive!

It slid across the surface like a molten oil slick.
　It ran down prey and predator, the quiet and the quick.
　The killdeer couldn't trick it, it was cinders in a flash.
The bones of all who faced it soon lay smoking in the ash.

　The antelope and cricket, the rattlesnake and bee,
　　The butterfly and badger, the coyote and the flea.
　　It was faster than the rabbit, faster than the fawn,
　They danced inside the dragon's mouth like puppets . . . then
　　were gone.

It offered up no quarter and burned for seven days.
　A hundred thousand acres were consumed within the blaze.
　Brave men came out to kill it, cutting trail after trail
But it jumped their puny firebreaks and scattered 'em like quail.

　It was ugly from a distance and uglier up close
　　So said the men who saw the greasy belly of the ghost.
　　It made'm cry for mama. Blistered paint on D-8 Cats.
　It sucked the sweat right off their backs and broke their
　　thermostats.

It was hotter than a burning brake, heavy as a train,
　It was louder than the nightmare screams of Abel's brother, Cain.
　It was war with nature's fury unleashed upon the land
Uncontrollable, enormous, it held the upper hand.

　The men retrenched repeatedly, continuously bested
　　Then finally on the seventh day, like Genesis, it rested.
　　The black-faced firefighters stared, unable to believe.
　They watched the little wisps of smoke, mistrusting their reprieve.

They knew they hadn't beaten it. They knew beyond a doubt.
   Though News Break *told it different, they knew it just went out.*
   Must'uv tired of devastation, grew jaded to the fame,
Simply bored to death of holocaust and walked out of the game.

You can tell yourself, That's crazy. *Fire's not a living thing.*
   It's only chance combustion, there's no malice in the sting.
   You can go to sleep unworried, knowing man is in control,
That these little freaks of nature have no evil in their soul.

But rest assured it's out there and the powder's always primed
   And it will be back, you know it . . . it's only biding time
   Till the range turns into kindling and the grass turns into thatch
And a fallen angel tosses out a solitary match.

Ah, the basic differences between men and women. Political correctness aside, some things never change.

CHAUVINIST? WHO ME?

When I suggested she do dishes and later stoke the fire
  Because I felt that was her proper place
She calmly took the custard pie and the plate of pickled beets
  And used it to redecorate my face!

Now I know this sounds unsavory in this modern day and age
  When male sensitivity is in
But I think it's biological, congenital at best,
  'Cause women see things differently than men.

Like the importance of a curtain or fragrance in the air
  Or, yes, the omnipresent potted plants.
They concern themselves with beauty and a certain ambience
  While I'm content to spray the place for ants!

In fairness to my jackass friends, it's not true that we don't care.
  We're lookin' from a different point of view.
And to illustrate my reasoning and perhaps to shed some light
  I offer this example as a clue.

I was sitting with a couple when I heard the man remark,
  "My dear, I think I've seen that dress before."
"Yes, you have. I was wearing it the last time we went out.
  Three years ago, or maybe it was four."

Then she chastised him severely and I'm sure she had a point,
  And I'll admit her wisdom right up front.
But my simple cowboy logic led me down a different path
  Like blind men feelin' up the elephant!

If women understood our thinkin' they might cut us all some slack
  And maybe their attitude might soften.
When he recognized his spouse's dress, the thought occurred to
    me. . . .
  The crazy fool's takin' her out too often!

The cat's name was Oreo.

WOMEN!

She cried over the cat. After all that had happened, she cried over the dang cat.

Christmas had been hectic. Feeding and watching out for twelve relatives for five days. Then in January when the blizzard hit I was at the state capital for a committee meeting. The power was out at the ranch and the water was off for forty-eight hours. She and the hired man managed to feed the cows but we lost four of them anyway. When I finally got through to her on the phone she said they were managing but hurry home if I could.

We held our little bull sale. She did the programs, mailed the flyers, planned the lunch, and smiled at prospective buyers for a day and a half. It went smoothly but she didn't get much rest that week.

It rained in March. The new calves got the scours. I was calvin', so she sorta took over treating the calves. She divided her time between haulin' the kids back and forth to town and nursin' sick calves.

Right before the regional track meet our oldest broke his leg. He was bitterly disappointed and was bedridden for two weeks. She waited on him hand and foot.

At our brandin' she fed thirty-four people outta the back of the pickup in the far pasture.

The first day it got over eighty-five degrees she went to town for parts. On the way home her car broke down and she walked the last four miles. Her Crock-Pot shorted out and the beans froze to the bottom. That was the night the school superintendent dropped by.

Well, she finally went to the doctor about the pain in her hands. Arthritis. Sorta what she'd suspected all along. Gettin' older.

In the last six months we've had two car wrecks, the well pump went out, my mother came to live with us, we found a leak in the roof above the kitchen sink, gophers got in her garden, the meat freezer gave up the ghost, I sold her favorite cow, our insurance went up, I started takin' high blood pressure pills, and they canceled her favorite TV show.

It's been kind of a tough go at our place these last few months. But she never complained. Just bowed her back and kept goin'.

We had company last night. After they left this morning, we found the cat dead in the driveway. A black tomcat. One of the barn cats. I didn't even know she cared about him. He never came in the house.

I found her in the bedroom cryin' her eyes out. "The cat?" I asked. She nodded. I held her.

Women cry over the strangest things.

When God reaches out and thumps hardheaded people behind the ear it makes 'em sit up and pay attention. I can imagine how Saul felt on the road to Damascus.

TOLERANCE

When our opinions get as immovable as a granite outhouse, God has a way of shaking the foundation.

I was searching for an artist who could lend just the right feeling to a book I was putting together. I found such a person. He lived in a remote mountain town and had no phone. With the help of the local postmistress and after several letters, he agreed to illustrate my book.

Besides his unique artistic style, he was a good cowboy. Over the months of correspondence and our occasional visits on his local pay phone, I developed a genuine liking and respect for him.

We agreed to meet at the Cowboy Poetry Gathering in Elko, Nevada.

I arrived Thursday night and began to test the limits of my envelope! I had the makin's of a personal best brewing when I spied an old friend, a big man whose effort had done much to promote cowboy poetry. I shook his hand warmly. It was then I noticed he was wearing a little short ponytail. I was overcome! I dressed him down for his uncowboy fashion statement and finished by removing the decorative ribbon binding his furry polyp!

Just then I felt a tap on the shoulder. I turned and a young man reached to shake my hand. He was decked out in his buckaroo finest. He introduced himself and remarked that he enjoyed my work. He explained that he was an actor.

As he talked, I focused on his earring. Earring! I became incensed! I lectured him on manly pride and ended up trying to bite off his earlobe.

In retrospect it occurred to me that I might have overreacted. Fortunately, these good fellows merely escaped my grasp rather than permanently disfiguring me.

The next day I was walking through the crowd when I heard a voice call my name. I turned. A hand pressed into mine and the voice said, "Hi, I'm yer new artist!"

He had blond hair braided into a pigtail that reached his waist. Eight—count 'em, eight!—earrings decorated his left ear!

I was dumbfounded.

He continued, "I'd like you to meet my wife." I looked to his side, where an attractive woman stood wearing a bowler hat and a gold ring in her nose!

Looking back, I suspect God set me up. He said to Himself, "This boy needs a lesson in tolerance." He was right. I was due.

I appreciate that I live in a world that is different from the world of most public radio contributors. I submitted this "true story" thinking it was probably too "cowy." Morning Edition ran it anyway, and I still have listeners ask me about it. (A little veterinary note: "Quills" are small tubes that are inserted temporarily in the teats to allow the udder to drain.)

CAUGHT IN THE ACT

They were nearly on top of him when he heard the sound of their hoofbeats. John glanced over his shoulder to see his foreman and the absentee owner fast approaching. He knew that the situation looked suspicious. He and Joe were standing over the stretched-out cow, each grasping a teat and naked as a jaybird!

They were covered from hair to spur with a sticky dripping coat of warm milk. John grinned like a possum eatin' bottle caps! His face cracked. "I can explain . . ."

Eastern New Mexico is a big place. John and his brother worked on an outfit that ran 55,000 acres and had only two corrals!

The boss had sent 'em out to find a certain cow that had calved. He'd spotted a calf who was doin' poorly and figgered they better check the mother. Shouldn't take 'em long, the pasture was only 9,000 acres!

They rode all morning to no avail. At midday they stopped at a tank dam and agreed a quick dip would improve their spirits. Joe's dog agreed.

They peeled off and jumped in. Under the surface the water was cool. As they lay there plotting their next move, up over the dam came the very cow they were hunting. Her bag was tight and all four teats stuck out like a helium glove. The calf bumped along behind her.

She spooked. The boys leaped out and sprang to the saddle. They made a wild chase and John got a rope around her head. Joe heeled her and they stretched her out.

With his horse pullin' back, John dismounted and began to milk out the ol' darlin'. She was sore and tight. After three or four squirts, he directed a stream at brother Joe. Joe took several direct hits, set his parkin' brake, and dove into the fray!

They stood there, each armed with two full quarters, and proceeded to drench each other like demented firemen marking out their territories.

It was about then that company appeared.

"We're just fixin' to put in the quills," offered John.

The owner stared at them like he had never seen this ancient high plains ritual performed by natives in authentic costume.

The foreman just shook his head.

The dog saw his chance and went to lickin' John like a giant Popsicle.

It is usually my practice to memorize any poem I write that has "potential." Potential, to me, means it might work its way into my live program. I did not commit "Rudolph's Night Off" to memory.

Morning Edition *ran the poem early in December on a Tuesday, as I recall. By Friday, we had received over five hundred requests for copies, which means the listeners had to call their local public radio stations, get the number of NPR headquarters in Washington, D.C., call them, get my number, and then call me. Matter of fact, I called NPR later that week and the recorded message said, "You have reached National Public Radio, if you want a copy of Baxter's poem please call . . ." And they gave my phone number.*

I'm not sure of "Rudolph's" appeal, but it does go to show you that the poet is often not the best judge of his own work.

RUDOLPH'S NIGHT OFF

'Twas the night before Christmas and Rudolph was lame!
The vet from the North Pole said, "Footrot's to blame.
I'll give him some sulfa, it's the best I can do,
But stall rest is needed the next week or two."

"Great Scott!" *cried old Santy, he turned with a jerk.*
"I won't git through Pierre if my headlight don't work!
On Interstate 40 I'll surely get fined
and lost in Montana if I'm flying blind!

"No cop in his right mind would give any clout
to a geezer who claimed that his reindeer went out!"
He gathered the others, ol' Donner and Blitzen,
were any among 'em whose nose was transmitzen?

They grunted and strained and sure made a mess
but no noses glowed brightly or ears luminesced.
"It's bad luck in bunches," *cried Santy, distressed.*
"We'll fly Continental, the Red-Eye Express!

"I'll just check the schedule." *He put on his glasses*
when up stepped ol' Billy, the goat from Lampasas.
He shivered and shook like a mouse on the Ark
but his horns were a beacon. . . . They glowed in the dark!

Santy went crazy! He asked "Why?" *with a smile.*
"I just ate a watch with a radium dial!
Where I come from in Texas we don't have thick hide.
My skin is so thin it shines through from inside."

"If that's true then let's feed him!" *cried Santy with glee.*
"Gather everything burnin' and bring it to me!"
So Billy ate flashbulbs and solar collectors,
electrical eels and road sign reflectors,

Firecracker sparklers, a Lady Schick shaver,
and Lifesavers, all of 'em wintergreen flavor,
Jelly from phosphorescellous fish,
Day-Glo pizza in a glittering dish,

Fireflies and candles and stuff that ignites,
then had him a big bowl of Northering Lights!
He danced on the rug and petted the cat
and after he'd finished and done all of that

To store up the static 'lectricity better
they forced him to eat two balloons and a sweater!
When he opened his mouth, light fell on the floor
like the fridge light comes on when you open the door!

4 5

His Halloween smile couldn't be better drawn
when he burped accident'ly, his high beams kicked on!
"Hitch him up!" cried ol' Santy, and they went on their way.
I remember that Christmas to this very day,

The sky was ablaze with the stars shining bright.
They were shooting and falling all through the night.
And I realize now, though my fingers are crossed
what I really was seein' . . . was ol' Billy's exhaust!

My paternal grandma, Ida, was born in 1878 in Sedalia, Missouri, to Mr. and Mrs. Christian Marti, Swiss immigrants. They went to Oklahoma Territory when she was a little girl. At age seventeen she married Baxter Black (age twenty-nine), who had come up from Bonham, Texas. They had six children (who lived past childhood). I am the descendant of her youngest (born 1918), who was named after the doctor who delivered him in her bedroom. He was the only child she had with a doctor in attendance.

GRANDMA'S PICTURE BOX

Grandma had a picture box. It was just like a time machine. Every year when we'd visit her in Oklahoma I'd spend hours lookin' through the old photographs. There were pictures of people I'd never seen . . . old-lookin' people with button-up shoes and big moustaches. And there were pictures of people I recognized, but they were different, younger than I knew them to be.

They'd be loose-stackin' hay on a big wagon or swimmin' in the tank. There was Uncle Leonard with his team of horses, the family lined up with their musical instruments, Grandpa rockin' on the front porch holdin' two little boys. I was the one on the left. A picture of my dad standin' beside ol' Ring wearin' Uncle Jake's hat and holdin' his pistol. The pistol was bigger than he was. Uncle Wade's Model T, Uncle Dink and Uncle Bert on a double date.

Grandma would sit with me sometimes. It took a lot longer to look at pictures with her 'cause there was a story with each photo.

"This is a picture of yer Grandpa with his twin brother, Barker. They could sure play music. I liked it, but I never let 'em play fer dances . . . wasn't Christian. And this is yer dad the year he got cold biscuits in his Christmas stocking. Went to town with fifty cents to buy gifts and spent it all on himself. He was five years old."

"Is that you, Grandma?"

"Yep. I was seventeen and had just started teachin' school in the Territory. The old schoolhouse was seven miles east and two south of here."

Even as I grew up I'd always get Grandma to give me a tour of old times. There were so many pictures that there were always stories I hadn't heard. She lived into her eighties in a house with no runnin' water and a big feather bed. She read her Bible every day and ate the fat off all us kids' fried ham.

She had fourteen grandchildren, but I was the only one named after Grandpa, so I thought I was special. She'd send each of us a Christmas card with a dollar bill in it. I haven't gotten one of those cards for many years now, but I'm thinkin' about her as I'm gettin' ready for Christmas with my own family. Maybe I'll get out her box of old pictures and take a private tour.

She'd be pleased if I did, I think. Merry Christmas, Grandma. I miss ya.

The first good job I had (after sackin' groceries) was on a sheep research facility at New Mexico State University. I was a student. My part wasn't very technical. I was the sheep holder. The boss would say, "Hold that sheep!" and I would.

After graduating from vet school I eventually worked for a large livestock company headquartered in Idaho. In addition to feedlots and cow calf operations, they had 20,000 range ewes. So I have spent a lot of time around cowboys and sheep people and I think that qualifies me to make some observations.

This column stimulated a nice response and is one of those that people still ask about.

SHEEPMEN, BORDER COLLIES, AND MULES

What do sheepmen, border collies, and mules have in common with cowboys, horses, and blue heelers? Nothing! Except that I've seen each one of 'em on all fours at one time or another, they seem to have nothing in common.

They are two distinct groups of species that are as different as mint jelly and Co-op dog food. Back in the Pleistocene Age, *Homo carnivorous* came to an evolutionary fork in the road. One group, staff in hand, took its livestock and beasts of burden and walked left. The other, rope in hand, headed west astride its beast of burden, accompanied by its livestock and pets.

Think back on the mules you have known personally. Did you ever know a stupid one? No. Did you ever know a stubborn, sly, mean, or snobbish one? Probably. People don't really own mules. They are like cats. They're livin' at your place and doin' as little as they can to get by and still stay there. A mule operates at about the same belligerence level as a cowman, which explains why the two don't get along. A sheepman will tolerate a smart ass as long as he'll pull the camp or pack the pots and pans. The cowboy insists on showing the mule who's boss.

Horses, on the other hand, have more frivolous personalities that bother sheepmen. Fun, in any form, makes sheepmen nervous. Did I say nervous? That brings us to one of the most amazing genetic creations on earth, the border collie. With the energy of a hummingbird, the work ethic of a boat person, and the loyalty of Lassie, they are miraculous animals. The more complicated the signals, the more uncooperative the livestock, the more they like it. Instinct and endless hours of training required by dog and master make them ideally suited for each other. They are as serious as a root canal!

The cowboy has no patience for the details of dog training. He didn't take much schooling to be a cowboy, so he figgers the blue heeler shouldn't need much training to be a cowdog. It's sort of a "hike it to me and go out for a pass" type of working relationship. Giving a good border collie to a cowboy would be like giving a Taiwanese socket set to a caveman.

But what happens when a rancher decides to raise both sheep and cattle? A mutant is created. He becomes uncertain. The sheep side of his brain keeps telling him to vote Republican, go to educational meetings, eat the heel, and pay cash. The cowboy side of his brain keeps saying, "I've got all my money in long-term CDs but I'd like something a little less risky. . . . I think I'll buy a racehorse."

It is a common fate among corporate employees to get laid off. I have noticed that many who fall victim to this fate (including me) have business cards printed that list their occupation as "consultant." Which they remain until they get another job.

My uncle Leonard told me the punch line I used in this poem.

THE CONSULTANT

Bein' in between jobs ain't no picnic.
  In fact, it's downright insultant.
  So I printed some cards, put signs in the yard,
    And bingo, became a consultant!

I solicited quality rest stops
  In search of the right clientele.
  Passed out ballpoint pens to all of my friends,
    Got an answer machine from Ma Bell.

At last an ol'timer sought my advice.
  He brought in his last balance sheet.
  I saw with a smile his management style
    Was outdated and obsolete.

So I set out to solve all his problems.
  I spoke like a preacher possessed!
  He sat there amazed, his eyes sorta glazed,
    I could see he was truly impressed.

He said not a word as I rambled on.
  For effect, I went over it twice.
  When time had expired, he politely inquired,
    "How much for this expert advice?"

I said, "Fifty bucks." I thought it was fair.
From his looks I thought I could fake it.
But he nodded his head and finally said,
"Well, son, I don't think I'll take it!"

Tink is one of my closest friends. He's been around and is a great storyteller. He makes me laugh till I am poundin' the floor and beggin' him to quit.

DEER RASSLIN'

Bulldoggin' deer has always been a risky undertaking. As a vet student, a brand-new semidumb starvin' freshman vet student, I volunteered for the deer rasslin' team. Dr. Davis kept several bucks in captivity. He monitored them for a variety of reasons. Once a week he would draw a blood sample for his studies.

The procedure was simple. The deer rasslin' team—Jay O, Jim, Bill, Foxy, and I—would enter a ten-by-twenty-foot pen with high walls. Using a combination of judo, heavy petting, and Olympic diving techniques, we would subdue bucks with antlers like a Radio Shack transmitter. It was like tryin' to tackle a swing set inside a moving school bus!

It was not a thinking man's job. But Tink had us beat by a mile. When he was a teenager in South Texas, his family managed a hunting camp. Hunters would come from the city for a weekend to hunt and enjoy the great outdoors.

Tink and his brother had been practicin' bulldoggin' deer. They had an ol' fifties model Jeep station wagon. Part of their territory included a large wheat pasture surrounded by an eight-foot deer fence. They'd start a buck runnin' down the fence, Tink would sit out on the fender, and when they got even with the deer, Tink would leap off and dog him!

They were braggin' to a new bunch of hunters about their prowess one night. Of course, no one believed 'em, so they decided to demonstrate.

Off they went, the ol' station wagon full of curious hunters. They spotted a deer, Tink mounted the bumper, and they hurtled down the fence line in pursuit!

As they drew alongside, Tink's feet slipped, and instead of catapulting onto the moving deer, he went over the front.

The Jeep ran right flat over him!

He rolled underneath, eating a mouthful of sand and bangin' his head on the muffler. Time stopped for an instant as he waited for the rear tires. He didn't have long to wait.

It took the Jeep a minute to get stopped and turned around.

"Are you hurt?" asked his brother, shinin' the flashlight over the mud grip tracks crossing Tink's legs and chest.

They helped him up. He tried to walk.

"Somethin's wrong. I must be hurt bad," he said as he stumbled around in the dirt.

They sorta balanced him between 'em, but every time he took a step he'd grimace. "Mighta broke my ankles," he said. They shined the light on the poor boy's boots.

It wasn't his ankles, his legs, or even his back. He'd broke the heels off both his boots!

I wrote this on the twenty-fifth wedding anniversary of one of my good friends.

JUST FRIENDS

I can't remember his number.
     I don't call him often enough.
His birthday always escapes me
     'cause I don't keep up with that stuff.

     And I'm lucky if I see him
          even once or twice a year
     But I'm really not complainin'
          'cause we're still close, we're just not near.

I recognize his daughter's voice.
     I remember when she was born.
Hell, I was there when he got married!
     I held the ring his wife has worn

     For all these years, his darlin'.
          Ya know, she hasn't changed a bit.
     And him and me? We're markin' time
          by the bad habits that we quit.

Together we're ambidextrous!
     Although we're really not a pair
We've got each other covered
     and, between us, a full head of hair!

We're part of each other's gristle,
*   as inveterate as bone.*
It's nice how life can fix it
*   so you don't have to go it alone.*

As I sit here blowin' smoke rings
*   from the pipe dreams that we've had,*
I'm wonderin' if I've told him
*   how many times it's made me glad*

Just to know he's out there somewhere,
*   like a dollar in my shoe,*
And how much it would please me
*   if he felt the same way, too.*

When I add up all my assets,
*   he's one thing I can't appraise.*
What's a promise or a handshake
*   or a phone call worth these days?*

It's a credit with no limit,
*   it's a debt that never ends*
And I'll owe him till forever
*   'cause you can't be more than friends.*

This true story explains how close I came to never becoming the "former large animal veterinarian" you know today. By the way, I have kept my promise.

TRIGGERNOMETRY

The sixty seconds that changed my life.

I suspect everybody has one. A chance meeting, a tragedy, a windfall, a lucky ride, a forgiveness, a walk down the aisle. Saul got his on the road to Damascus. Freckles Brown got his on Tornado, Nixon got his when the tape shredder broke, and I got mine in a classroom in the spring of 1965.

I had started college majoring in animal husbandry. I enjoyed two good years judging livestock, rodeoing, playing music, and studying the science of agriculture. The summer of '64 I got antsy and decided to take a shot at veterinary school. This required that I take some courses that I normally would have avoided like a house cat avoids Co-op dog food.

Looming ahead of me were two semesters of physics, two semesters of organic chemistry, and one five-hour course of calculus and trigonometry. I felt like Gutzon Borglum standing in front of Mount Rushmore with a garden trowel.

I put off the dreaded math course and dove headfirst into the chemistry and physics. Unfortunately, the pool was drained! The only people who didn't seem to mind my difficulty were on the local draft board. To hedge my odds I visited the navy recruiter. He gave me a test and a physical. I postponed his invitation.

By the second semester I was sinking like a set of car keys. I had squeaked by so far and applied to vet school. I was now taking chemistry, physics, and the math course intended for Albert Einstein!

In February the navy checked me again. By March I had a 54 average in math (passing was 60). In April I received the letter from vet school. I had been accepted! Contingent on my completing the required courses. I started going to math class like a born-again algebra teacher. Monday through Friday plus a four-hour review every Saturday. It was like getting your prostate examined six days a week.

The day final grades were posted I checked chemistry . . . a C, physics . . . a D, math . . . flunked it flatter'n a hammered brownie! The Saturday review teacher's assistant was in her office. I stood in line to talk to her. The student in front of me was complaining about his grade. He'd gotten a B! When my turn came I fell to my knees in front of the harried graduate student. I can still see her . . . worn sandals, a chipped toenail, flaky skin on her shins, a peasant dress, straight hair, and John Denver glasses. I looked up her nostrils and she said, "Yes?"

I rapidly explained my predicament; I had to pass her class or I wouldn't be accepted to veterinary school. She glanced at her paper, fingered her peace symbol, and peered down at the pitiful figure groveling at her feet. The people in line behind me looked away in disgust.

"You got a fifty-eight."

"Yes, ma'am, I know."

"You also flunked the final."

"Yes, ma'am, I know," I pleaded, "but I did the best I could. I was here every Saturday, as regular as an insulin shot." She paused. I held my breath.

"I'll pass you on one condition."

I looked her in the eye and said, "Anything!" I could picture myself doing her laundry all summer or chewing buffalo hides to make her new sandals.

Time froze . . .

"If you promise never to take calculus or trigonometry again."

I kissed her stickery ankles. She said, "Next."

Dogs. I love dogs.

ONEUPSMANSHIP

No tellin' how many good dogs he outlived,
　No matter how good your dog was
　　He'd once had a collie, a heeler or gyp
　　　That did everything your dog does

And more! The same for horses and pickup trucks
　Though the one he drove was a wreck.
　　The best I could tell, he didn't have nothin'
　　　But I've never seen that affect

His opinion on anything you mighta owned
　From a purebred bull to a bit!
　　By the time he'd finished pontificatin',
　　　You'd wind up suckin' hind tit!

Last night I was braggin' on one of my dogs
　I'd sold at the top of the year
　　To a herder who worked on Basabe's ranch.
　　　They said my dog had no peer.

It was seven miles of circuitous road
　From the lower field to the lane.
　　They'd send my good collie to bring the sheep home
　　　And never had call to complain.

He'd start 'em out where the new highway sign warned,
CAUTION: LIVESTOCK CROSSING AHEAD,
Then herd 'em north to the Conoco billboard,
Go right till a homemade sign read,

POLOMBO'S TOMATOES AND VEGETABLE STAND,
Where he'd turn toward the four-way stop.
Platteville read EAST, so he'd go till he spotted
DICK'S WELDING AND SHEET METAL SHOP.

Take a left on Bromley then up past the barn
That advertised HAY BY THE BALE,
Till at last he turned up the Willow Creek Road
By the sign that said, RABBITS FOR SALE.

At the third mailbox sayin', BASABE SHEEP
He'd fetch 'em just like he'd been shown
And drive that big bunch of scatterbrained woolies
Up the lane, just him, all alone.

"Top that!" I thought, "You cranky ol' coot!" He said,
"That's mighty impressive indeed!
Though I'm not surprised 'cause my dog spent last year
Teachin' all them sheep how to read!"

THE ROPIN' VET

Louie used to buy horses for the feedlot. Whenever he'd find a good stout one that was deaf and looked like it could tread mud, he'd send it our way. I'd usually check 'em over, float their teeth, deworm 'em, vaccinate 'em, and change their oil. Occasionally he sent one with no faults, but I was only there ten years, so I never saw that one!

Feedlot number three called one morning to say Louie'd delivered a new horse to the yard. As I pulled up to the horse barn I called Louie on the radio to ask about any "peculiarities." I'd learned from past experience that all arrived with a flaw of some kind . . . some minor, some fatal.

"Louie, what can you tell me 'bout the new horse?"

"You'll like him, Doc. Gentle as a puppy. Sound, maybe twelve years old, big'un . . . sixteen hands. Belonged to a little old lady who only rode him to the senior center once a week."

I waited.

"Oh, by the way, he's a little hard to catch."

In the first pen stood Whitey. He had a gentle look in his eye. I walked right up to him. He backed off. I coaxed, wheedled, cooed, and clucked him round and round the corral.

Now, as any vet can tell ya, I didn't hire on to train 'em! Just to doctor 'em!

I ran outta patience, threw down the halter, and got out my rope! Although there are exceptions, most vets are not good ropers. It's like givin' a typewriter to a cephalopod! I roped the post, the hayrack, the back rubber, the barn door, the two horses with him, and finally caught him astraddle the water tank.

Years later I still haven't learned my lesson. To this day I carry a rope and act like I can use it.

Dr. Huey down in Tennessee is smarter'n me. He went out to look at an ol' tobacco farmer's sick calf.

"He's in the pasture, Doc. You're young, you can catch him."

Dr. Huey dug his rope outta the truck and started swingin' it. He knocked the old man's hat off before it finally hung up on the sideview mirror.

"You any good with that?" asked the old man suspiciously.

"Not too, but it don't make much difference," said Dr. Huey. "I charge a dollar a throw whether I catch 'em or not."

The old man yelled over his shoulder, "Leroy, git out there and catch that calf for the good doctor!"

In the years since this piece ran I have had it confirmed often. The tale of this bull's holiday has become standard grist for livestock haulers around the country. If it is told often enough I guess it will enter the exalted realm of fiction. (For the Spanish deprived ... without cojones *means he would no longer be a* toro.)

THE HERD SIRE

This is one of those stories that sounds so unbelievable that you'll know I didn't make it up.

Mike studied the bloodlines. He checked performance records. He knew his herd like the top two layers of his toolbox. He was a good young cattleman.

When he decided on a course of action to improve his herd's genetics he called the breed association rep. They discussed his needs. Plans were made for the fieldman to attend a bull sale in Texas with the express instructions to buy exactly the right bull.

The call from Texas delighted Mike. The fieldman had bought half interest in the perfect yearlin' bull that would carry Mike's cows into the twenty-first century. For $10,000.

He agreed that the co-owner, a purebred breeder from Oklahoma, could use the bull that fall. Then he would ship him to the Pine Ridge country of northwestern Nebraska in time for Mike's spring breeding.

In February arrangements were made to put the bull on the back of a load going as far as Sterling, Colorado. The trucker would call Mike on arrival.

Mike waited anxiously. Several days passed and nobody called. He called his partner only to find they'd left Oklahoma territory a week before.

Feeling uneasy, Mike called the Sterling sale barn. "No. No," they didn't remember any bull. "Let us check." They suggested possibly the bull Mike was lookin' for had been bought by a trader.

"What'd he pay?" asked Mike.

"Fifty-six cents a pound."

In a panic he tracked down the trader. He'd run the bull through the Brush sale. The trader said he broke even. Packerland had bought him as a baloney bull.

Mike drove all night to Packerland in a desperate effort to save his bull. No, they said, he was too thin to kill so they'd sent him to a feedlot in Rocky Ford.

Mike smelled like burnin' rubber and was chewin' the upholstery when he boiled into the feedlot in a cloud of dust. The foreman was surprised but led him over to the receiving pens. There stood Mike's future; road weary, coughin', and covered with sale barn tags.

Mike's knees were shakin'.

"Nice bull," said the foreman, "but ya cut 'er close, sonny. Tomorrow evenin' he'da looked a lot different without his horns and *cojones*."

I have spent my life working in the livestock business. Today I have cattle on feed (in a feedlot) and each spring I buy a few old gummers to calve out. My daughter has become a good hand with cows and a fine horseman. It is the way of my people.

So there has never been anything sacrosanct about vegetarianism to me. Yet I do respect people who become zealots in their defense. It takes tremendous willpower to stick to a strictly vegetarian diet. I had a friend who was a vegetarian. She ate a lot of candy.

This commentary and the one following it are meant in good spirit; but in the case of cowboys and vegetarians it is the truth in humor that makes it funny.

THE COWBOY'S GUIDE TO VEGETARIANS

In an effort to foster an understanding between cowboys and vegetarians, it is crucial to debunk certain myths.

Myth #1. Vegetarians are all left-wing, liberal Democrats who were hippies in the '60s

Not so. The average age of a 1991 vegetarian is thirty-five. So in 1964 they would have been eight years old. They were being forced to clean their plate ("But Mom, I don't like broccoli!") before they could have dessert.

It was not until President Bush came out of the closet and announced his dislike of broccoli that he found a cause some vegetarians could rally behind. Three registered as Republicans!

Myth #2. Vegetarians are a vanishing breed

An interesting myth. They are holding their own, approximately 3 percent of the U.S. population. But the turnover is high. The percentage is also affected by immigrants, ethnic minorities, and the poor. As they improve their lifestyle they feed their families more meat.

In a constant effort to maintain their ranks, vegetarians align themselves with like-minded groups who might help them vegetate; New Wave trade shows, psychic conventions, and the Hare Krishna.

Myth #3. Most vegetarians became vegetarians because their mothers said liver was good for them

As good a reason as any, but not necessarily so. Snoopy, Garfield, and Mickey had more influence than mom. These were animals who ate chocolate chip cookies and lasagna. They could sing and knew Annette Funicello. They could speak and go to heaven. It followed that Porky Pig and Foghorn Leghorn had human feelings too and didn't relish being eaten. Vegetarians feel sorry for drumsticks and bacon bits.

Myth #4. All vegetarians are alike

Wrong again! Some vegetarians eat fish and chicken. (The reasoning here escapes me. Maybe their cuddle factor is low?)

Others will eat only eggs and milk. That's a practical decision, I suspect. One can pass up a Spam sandwich or a bowl of menudo, but it's not so easy to turn down chocolate mint ice cream.

And there is a small group of believers who eschew even the wearing of wool or leather. They are easily identified wearing petrochemical derivatives and a plastic shower cap.

STAY TUNED TOMORROW FOR: A Vegetarian's Guide to Cowboys!

We got a call from the editor of a magazine called Vegan Magazine.
I sent her a copy, but I don't think they ran it.

A VEGETARIAN'S GUIDE TO COWBOYS

Many myths have been promulgated that have fostered a misunderstanding of cowboys by herbivores. It is incumbent on me to shed some light on this subject for my vegetarian listeners.

Myth #1. Cowboys are mean to cows

This myth may be reinforced by the cowboy's habit of roping cows for sport, branding their young, and primping them like poodles at livestock shows. But in their defense, these practices are done without malice. Just sort of the usual predator/ prey relationship, like parents with children enrolled in organized sports.

Myth #2. Cowboys are right-wing political fanatics

Cowboys are suspicious of politicians and, like most Americans, don't vote either. They hold to a muddled Code of the West that forbids associating with known feminists but allows kissing your horse. Very confusing.

Myth #3. Cows hate cowboys

Cows have an IQ somewhere between a cedar post and a sandhill crane. It is unlikely that they lay awake nights plotting revenge. However, fate has made the cow and cowboy dependent on each other. It's the same unnatural relationship that exists between politicians and newspaper reporters, or lawyers and criminals.

Myth #4. Cowboys are a vanishing breed

As long as 97 percent of the population eats meat, there will be cows, and as long as there's cows, there will be cowboys. However, they *are* hard to see from the freeway.

Myth #5. Cowboys eat beef every day

Or buffalo wings, pig's feet, or cheek meat off an old ewe. They'll even eat hay if you put enough whiskey on it. Actually, they'll eat most anything the cook serves up, though I've never seen 'em eat a snail darter or a spotted owl.

Myth #6. Cowboys are not like the romantic image portrayed in Marlboro commercials and John Wayne movies

Of course they are! 'Specially if you catch 'em between gettin' bucked off before breakfast and losin' their lunch on the way home from the dance.

I am a fan of stock dog trials. I admire those folks with the patience
and skill to train these dogs. Of course, every run is not perfect.

THE STOCK DOG DEMONSTRATION

P ete was invited to put on a working stock dog demonstration
at the agricultural fair in the nearby town of Perdue,
Saskatchewan. He could have brought his own lambs that
were "dog wise," but his hosts offered to furnish the sheep.

On arrival in Perdue that morning Pete peeked into the dark
trailer at the sheep. Six big black-headed Suffolk ewes glared back
at him malevolently. It was like looking into a cave full of bank
examiners. He stationed his wife, Pam, and his dog, Jock, at the
back and opened the tailgate. The ewes charged in a flying wedge
and bowled over the defense.

They made straight for the show barn, then turned at the last
second toward a windbreak of willers. Jock was on 'em, snapping
at their noses.

The ewes holed up in the windbreak . . . all save one, who
started down the highway to town. Pete sent Jock "away to me!" to
fetch 'er back. The two met three times on the center line before
she turned back for the bunch. She arrived with a bloody snoot
and led the others down the road in the opposite direction.

Assuming control, Pete, Pam, and Jock aimed for the intersec-
tion leading back to the fairgrounds. The road was fenced on both
sides except for one driveway that led to a nice country home set
back on a beautifully landscaped lawn. The ewes took a hard right
and made for the house.

As the flock rounded the corner of the house Pete caught a
glimpse of a well-dressed lady peeking through the curtain. They
made twelve passes around the house trampling shrubs, lawn, and

manicured flower beds. They mangled four bicycles and knocked over six flowerpots before panting to a slippery stop on the front porch. The porch floor looked like the bottom of a Dumpster. The white front door was streaked with blood, urine, snot, and other ovine by-products.

The enraged homeowner opened the door to register her displeasure. The lead ewe broke for the living room! Pete followed, slamming the door behind him.

They raced over sofas, coffee tables, potted plants; under the kitchen table; through the hall; and back to the living room, where the ewe paused to squat on the shag carpet (beige, of course) in front of the television set!

Pete caught a hind leg and drug her across the rug toward the door. Just as he opened his mouth to shout, "No, don't!" the helpful homeowner jerked open the door, admitting ewe number two.

In small towns like Perdue news travels fast. It was standing room only for the working stock dog demonstration that afternoon.

It seems that affluent civilizations go through fads regarding diet. At the time I wrote this poem, preservatives in food were the subject of tabloid headlines and fifteen-second in-depth sound bite analyses on TV.

If satire is "trenchant wit used for the purpose of exposing human folly," then this piece may qualify. I prefer to call it "turning over our sanctimonious stones and looking at the holes in the queen's underwear. Gently locating our flaws and foibles and wrapping them in hunter's fluorescent orange. Nudging that fine line between good taste and throwing up in your hat."

COWBOY PRESERVES

I've been searching for a reason as to why we live so long
Our life expectancy is hard to beat.
Some say it's easy livin' or medical research
But I think it's the preservatives I eat.

Preservatives are everywhere. You might just be surprised.
In mayonnaise and Roman Meal bread.
Smoked salmon, pickled herring, even some granola bars.
In margarine, the hard stick or the spread.

In diet pop and soy sauce and Kellogg's Special K,
The Aunt Jemima syrup that you bought.
In hot dogs and baloney and Betty Crocker cake mix
And Tang, the choice of every astronaut.

Oh, I eat roast beef and veggies, just to have a change of pace
Man cannot live on benzoates alone.
Yet I crave the magic tingle that I get from my Parkay
Or a Twinkie as it soaks into my bones.

My body now depends on the preservatives I eat.
I'm sure they retard spoilage of my brains.
I'll look forever youthful even through my twilight years
Because of their protection in my veins.

Someday I'll just be sittin' in my rocker on the porch
And everyone will say I'm lookin' great.
Because I'll be so well preserved, no one will know I'm dead
Unless they read my expiration date!

I received quite a few letters from pilots and aviators wanting copies of this piece to reprint. NPR also received a letter from a lady, which they read on the air. She was taking me to task for telling a story about hunting coyotes. Although I've not hunted them from an airplane, I have stalked them afoot many times. They are my favorite animal; stealthy, adaptable, clever, and prolific. They are the entrepreneur, the migrant worker, the pioneer, the unstoppable spirit of the average Joe who wants to better himself, which is also me. But sometimes our territories collide.

FEAR OF FLYING

Andy summed up flying the best I've heard: "If yer gonna have to land in a field, always land *with* the rows!"

Although I had a momentary lapse of good judgment once and took a week's worth of flying lessons, I have since left that task up to more serious folks, people who don't stay up all night celebrating and can actually reset the time on a digital watch.

I know cowboys who are pilots. It's a frightening combination, akin to a CPA who does nude modeling on the side. All they talk about is flying, and if there's two at your table, your brain goes numb after five minutes. It's like being trapped in a pickup on the road from Broadus to Billings between two cuttin' horse people!

But for good reason many western ranchers have taken up flying. They can check windmills, count cows, and chase coyotes without having to open a gate. Roy hired a local boy out of Chadron to pilot him over his ranch to thin out the coyote population. The plane was a single-engine Super Cub. The side door is dropped and the hunter straps himself in and leans out the door, cannon in hand. It is not a job for the fainthearted.

The pilot followed Roy's directions and was soon swooping down on the crafty coyotes while Roy blazed away with his twelve-gauge. Suddenly the plane began to shake like a wet dog! The vibration loosened Roy's upper plate, and the pilot's *"I'd Rather Be Flying"* T-shirt began to unravel! Roy, in his nearsighted exuberance, had led the coyote too much and shot the tip off of one propeller blade!

With heroic control, the young pilot landed the plane on an old stretch of rutted wagon road. He shut 'er down and staggered out into the sagebrush, visibly shaken.

He didn't care that he was twenty miles from the ranch headquarters and facin' a long walk back in the company of a crusty old rancher who had spit all over the side of his plane. He was just thankful to be on the ground!

His prayers were interrupted by an explosion. He dived for the dirt and smashed his new aviator sunglasses in the process. He looked back and Roy was standing in front of the plane, holding the smoking twelve-gauge.

"I evened 'em up, sonny. She ought to fly okay now." He'd shot the tip off the other end of the prop.

Did they make it home? You bet yer shirttail they did! It vibrated a little bit, but no worse than drivin' down a railroad track at a hundred miles an hour!

People who spend most of their workday outside often develop an intimate relationship with the weather. Springtime in the Rockies ain't all it's cracked up to be.

JANUARY, FEBRUARY, MUD

March comes in like a lion and goes out like a flatbed full of wet carpet. The most I can say about March is, it is a month of change. If March were a person, it would be an old man, cracked and weathered and cantankerous. Occasionally bearable but bent on maintaining his reputation for orneriness. The kind that won't turn up his hearing aid or zip his fly.

In the Deep South, March is pleasant. Matter of fact, they even look forward to it. But for most of cow country, the Deep South might as well be on the back side of the moon. The March rain up here is not a gentle, life-giving shower from Heaven to be savored and sniffed. It's more like the angels hosing out their hog-confinement shed!

And the gentle breezes that whisper through the Houston pine trees aren't even a distant relative to the steady, bone-chilling twenty-mile-an-hour wind that whistles across eastern Idaho.

Even the word *March* is harsh and conjures up a tough, unforgiving image. Not like light and airy April or comfortable, short February. If I was asked to rename March, I would call it Mud. January, February, Mud . . . Mud 7, 1992 . . . the Ides of Mud. Doesn't sound much different, does it?

Mud is a busy time of the year: feedlots are full, calvin' has started, and the lambin' crew is getting the jugs ready. Cowboys are still wearin' their winter long johns and five-buckle overshoes. It's too soon to take the mud and snows off the pickup. The days are gettin' longer but nobody knows why.

The horses still have their hairy side out. It is usually the last month you can stick a tractor up to the axle.

What most people do in March is look forward to April.

"Well, one good thing about this miserable wind is it'll help dry up the mud."

"We'll be able to get into the fields next month."

"The bulk of the calvin' will be over in three or four weeks."

It seems I ought to have somethin' good to say about March. It's good and cold, good and windy, and good and long. Is that good enough?

I only knew one cowman who liked March: McQuilken. He said when it was over at least he still wouldn't have the whole winter to go through. He was just glad it didn't come in November.

Boller was the first dog I had in Colorado. He was a year old when a friend of mine (named Boller) found him in a local tavern we call the Arm Pit. Somebody'd dumped him off. So my friend gave the dog to my wife and daughter while I was out of town. The dog was an Australian shepherd with one blue eye.

He's been shot and run over, broken a leg and a hip. But he was always there to keep me humble. I buried him in July '96. He was just a dog, but he'll be in my Heaven.

BOLLER'S COMMENTS

Whel frenz, I was ther. Bakster's buk pardy. He prefurrs I refur to him az Mastr wich emplys sum Roilty capasite. So far az ledership gose I'd rank him sumwher between Custer and Dookakuz.

So, he throes this BBQ to anowns his latest markitting asolt on the gollabul! I red sum ov it. At lest the pichurs ar gud. Hiz artist frends demonstraded wye thay mak a livin drowing insted of trhowin a rop!

His mother an stepfodder waz ther. He puit the ol man tar pappuring the wel howz. Hiz mother waz a soprise. I'd herd him tel peppel he was an orfan to get simpathe.

Bumbling Black mus be a pirromanyak! He etokd the campfhire with enuf wud to bild a hunting loge, then primd it with a galon of gass. He lit it an blu the hud offe his pikup!

By dark the blaz had burrnd doun to the ziz ov a smal apartmnt complx!

Garre shode up luking 4 a yoddeling dawg. I awdishunned but I'd breethd enuf sqmoke to fog ten akers of cotten, so he passed.

Then the muzishuns kam owt of the wud wirk! Bloogras. I kan tak it ore leve it! I hd to mak mye rowndz.

I finuly fownd the hors's. Thay were standing arownd on 3 leggs grumbulin abot the fier an makin fune of the roppers. Same confursachun I'd herd when I past the artist wivs.

I got bak. Peple were tryn to leve but Bax waz stil pating ther bak and pumping ther arm hopping thayd menchun hiz buk in ther nuz papper or tv sho. It wuz chamful!

Neckst morning tour plaz lukt lik DADE conty! Enuf glumanumm kans to resikle a spas shutul! The fier went owt 2 daz latr.

Things are bak to normal. I've got so mane bonz berryd arownd her it luks lik a helafunt gravyard! Ges I'm set for wintr. Prety gud pardy.

I'm a better man for knowin' Frank.

ANOTHER GOOD MAN GONE

I had just finished bein' on an Extension program in the Herington, Kansas, sale barn. I was standin' in the auction ring afterwards tryin' to answer a few questions and shake hands with the local stockman. My veterinary lecture, as usual, had been more humorous than informative.

One older gentleman waited till the last question had been asked, then he approached me and offered his hand. I didn't catch his name. He was wearin' thick glasses. He reached into his shirt pocket and handed me a Polaroid snapshot of a cowdog settin' in the back of an ol' Chevy pickup. "Go git in the pickup!" he said, an obvious reference to one of my stories. He laughed and wandered off.

A while later I wrote of meetin' him and of the snapshot. I was tryin' to explain why I enjoy makin' up poems and columns about people in our way of life. That ol' man, I said, was the reason I did it.

One day I got a letter from a lady who had read my story and she said that ol' man was her dad.

He and I struck up a friendship. We wrote occasional letters. He'd send me photos of his horse and grandkids. We'd visit on the phone. He'd talk about the old days. He'd cowboyed all his life and still helped on local gathers or checked pastures sometimes. He was in his eighties.

His health started slippin', so I went to see him. We had a good visit. Before I left he gave me a photo of Bill Pickett doggin' a steer. He took it off his kitchen wall. He claimed he'd seen Bill do his stuff. His wife gave me a wooden hot pad. She picked it right off the kitchen table and gave it to me.

His wife died. He sorta lost interest in things. We talked on the phone infrequently. He went into a nursing home.

The last time I called him, he was in and out of reality. He was ready, he said. He missed his wife terribly. He became incoherent.

"Call my daughter," he said, "she'll tell ya how I am." I told him I'd rather talk to him if I could.

"I'm not doin' good in the last stages," he said. Then his voice got strong as a bell and he said, "One of these days I'll be lookin' for that ol' black dog up in the white clouds." Then the nurse came on and said he couldn't talk anymore.

He died two days later. A good man. Just one of us who rode good horses, loved a good woman, and was true to his friends.

Too bad he can't send me a snapshot from Heaven. 'Course, I guess I don't need one. He already told me what it would be like.

My first few years doin' vet work in Idaho and Nevada often found me wandering the wilderness lookin' for some creek or set of corrals or rusty mailbox. But I soon realized that range country had neighborhoods just like in town. The people just live farther apart.

LOST

A source of pride amongst cowboys
  Is knowin' the lay of the land
And any poor fool that gets lost
  They figger ain't much of a hand!

  They said, "We'll meet up at Bull Crick."
    Then looked at me like a trainee.
  "Draw me a map and I'll find it.
    Columbus had nothin' on me."

Daylight broke into my windshield,
  Headed south and loaded for bear.
I turned at the Grasmere station
  I should'a shot myself right there!

  Nothin' was like they described it,
    No mailbox where it should be,
  No coyote hide on the fence post,
    Now where's Mary's Crick s'posed to be?

Their map showed tourist attractions
  Including, I swear, Noah's Ark!
Little ol' tricklin' Sheep Creek
  Was wider than Yellowstone Park.

I crossed the Cow and the Horse Crick
And cricks named for Nickles and Dimes
Through Nit Crick, Louse Crick and Crab Crick,
Crossed Willer Crick twenty-eight times!

I drove demented and crazy
A'chasin' my tail like a dog!
Coursing through desert and mountain,
Brush thicket and cattail bog.

Fighting back panic, I'm thinkin',
"I could die and never be found!
Worse yet, I'll look like a gunsel
Who can't find his way outta town!"

Harold was the boss of the truckers.
I figgered he might set me right.
So, I called him up on the two-way
And explained my desperate plight.

He said, "Describe yer surroundings."
I looked for a landmark somewhere.
"Ain't nothin' but rocks and sagebrush!"
He said, "Sonny, yer almost there!"

Ardel was a cattleman. One of our mutual friends, Judy, who tended
bar at a local watering hole, made the observation about Ardel that
became the punch line of this poem.

ARDEL'S BULL

Now Ardel's cows were all crossbred
        in the fullest sense of the word.
Part Hereford, Holstein, and llama
        and maybe some yak in the herd.

He had one ol' bramer confusion
        whose hide was loose as a goose
With a hump that flapped like a diaper
        and pendulous lips like a moose.

So, when he showed up at the bull sale
        we didn't expect him to buy
A genuine purebred herd sire.
        He wasn't that kind of a guy.

And we were right, at least for a while
        'cause he never bid over eight
The bulls were sellin' for twice that
        till lot number 12 hit the gate.

He had an obvious defect
        that showed on the front of his face.
One eye was blue as marble,
        the other stared out into space!

The bidding was apathetic.
> *The buyers were quiet as mice.*
So Ardel slid in like a coyote
> *and bought him at hamburger price.*

"Sold! Let 'im out, boys, he's finished!"
> *They took one last look at the ox*
Who stumbled over the sawdust
> *then bumped into the auctioneer's box!*

"Dang it, Ardel! What's the story?"
> *asked the ringman who stood by the door.*
"Well," *said Ardel,* "not complainin'
> I'd'uv paid considerably more

"To improve my herd's genetics
> But, in truth, he's the best I could find.
See, my cows are so dadgum ugly,
> I needed a bull that was blind!"

DOG EMOTIONS

It is my observation that dogs feel certain basic emotions like affection, fear, confusion, and joy. I'm not sure they're capable of feeling sadness or jealousy or if they can get their feelings hurt. But I believe a dog can get embarrassed!

Take the Sunbeam clippers to a long-haired dog and see if he doesn't slink off behind the barn.

We bought a few acres out in the country but rented in town till we built our house. Boller, my good cow dog and companion, stayed in the backyard but *lived* to go out to the place.

He would know when I was fixin' to leave. He'd wait by the front door vibratin' like a bowstring! I'd tease him a little, then say, "Go git in the pickup!" I'd open the door and he'd streak across the grass, across the driveway, and catapult up into the back of the pickup!

One winter morning I was preparing to drive out and split some wood. Boller was tuned up and tickin' like a two-dollar watch! I peeked out the door when I released him. We'd had an ice storm. The trees hung heavy with icicles and the concrete driveway was like a mirror. Boller shot across the frozen grass, reached the driveway, set his hind legs to spring skyward, hit the ice, and slid like a statue of a dog praying, flat into the side of the pickup!

He didn't know what happened. He glanced over his shoulder, saw me watching, and walked, red-faced, around the back of the pickup.

Bill said Booker was one of the dumber dogs they'd ever had on the ranch. He didn't have much cow dog in him, so, other than entertainment, he wasn't much use. To his credit, he did make an effort, but it was usually a disaster. Booker grew up to the sound of regular outbursts, curses, and colorful epithets directed his way.

One hunting season Bill and a friend winged a buck. They drove the truck as close to the brush as possible, then went looking.

Ever hopeful, Bill said, "Booker, find the deer!" Well, to everyone's amazement, big ol' slobberin' Booker found it!

Bill heaped praise on him. "Good dog! Good dog!"

Booker was so pleased he was beside himself. He grinned a big ol' loopy grin and was overcome with this unaccustomed acclaim. In his exuberance, he raced for the pickup, made an Olympic leap, cleared the entire bed, hooked his hind paw on the far side, and nose-dived into the dirt!

They found him up the road about a half a mile . . . acting like nothing happened.

3% MARKUP

Leonard was a man who appreciated the value of an education but he didn't let it stand in his way. He, himself, had completed the eighth grade and gone into the construction business. He was successful and became a wealthy man. In an interview with a high-finance business magazine, the reporter asked Leonard the secret of his success.

"Son," he said, "I allus charge a three percent markup. Anybody that can't make it on a three percent markup doesn't deserve to make it in business."

"Excuse me, sir," said the stunned reporter. "Nobody could possibly run an operation like yours on a three percent markup."

"Well, I do. I look at a pile of dirt, figger what it will cost to move it, and multiply that times three!"

Alvin had worked for Leonard more times than anybody else on the payroll. Leonard would fire him in a fit of frustration, then hire him back as soon as he needed a Cat skinner. Alvin had gotten into the habit of doin' a little work on the side. Between Leonard's scheduled construction site projects, Alvin would dig basements.

Alvin wouldn't take the job if it wasn't on the way. It took a skilled operator like him only a couple hours to dig a good basement. These excavations were done without Leonard's permission, but with his knowledge. Leonard didn't object. Not because Alvin had a big family and needed the extra income, but because after the basement was dug, the landowners would usually call him to build their house.

Leonard was on site one afternoon. The crew had come to a standstill. He stomped around in characteristic fashion and realized the dozer work was holdin' everybody up. Alvin was late. He was supposed to be bringin' the Cat from the last big construction site.

Leonard jumped in his car and started backtrackin'. He figgered Alvin had stopped to dig a basement along the way. Surenuf, he saw a pile of fresh dirt out on a grassy hillside.

He wound his car up the trail and spied Alvin sittin' on the track havin' a leisurely smoke. The thirty-ton bulldozer lay on its side like those pictures of the *Titanic*.

"Dagnabit, Alvin! Yer fired!" Leonard cussed like an oil patch veteran. "I've got two crews of men, thousands of dollars worth of machinery, and a politically important customer all come to a dead stop 'cause of you! What in the hillbilly heck do ya think yer doin'!"

Alvin looked at the beached bulldozer, then at Leonard. "Workin' for four-fifty an hour."

gregarious fellow who was bragging about his secret sea-
ipe one afternoon at the Denver Stock Show. He suggested
nake him a radio commercial. So I did. It wasn't what he
expec..l. But bein' the good sport he was, he used it anyway.

SECRET SEASONING

Sometimes it is embarrassing when your friends catch that
entrepreneurial spirit. How many times have you gently
tried to tell them that, sure, Amway's great, but what are ya
gonna do with all that soap in the closet? That you don't really
need a water filter, or that networking chain letters is not your bag.

I used to have a weakness for get-rich-quick schemes, but now I
feed cattle and dabble in Iraqi real estate.

Jim, a North Platte auctioneer and friend, was exploring the
marketing possibilities of his latest venture (which followed the
unsuccessful Starling Sanctuary and the pencils made of duck
feet). He planned to supplant Mutant Ninja Pizza as the greatest
thing since sliced cheese!

Jim's Secret Seasoning! To enhance your barbecue experience!
He closed his eyes as visions of secret seasoning blanketed the
earth like volcanic ash. You could almost smell the belch of Mount
St. Helens. "But we gotta have a gimmick," he said.

We ordered another round of Cactus Perrier and explored alternative uses. It should be, we figgered, the only secret seasoning
that could be bought by the yard, in bulk, like concrete or barley.
Delivered in a twenty-ton end dump direct to the spice rack or the
driveway!

It could be applied to icy sidewalks or intersections. One could
market it as a spray or cologne to be dabbed gently on the upper
lip or around the sweatband, wherever perspiration would bring
out its true essence.

Powder it in your shoes to prevent offensive odors. Or market it as an air freshener in the shape of a hog liver to be dangled from the rearview mirror.

Jim's secret seasoning could be used to disguise the real flavor of fruitcake, Metamucil, or airline food.

It could be served at cocktail parties, next to the punch bowl, in a fifty-pound block!

The list for potential uses was endless: tanning hides, pickling fatback, wart removal, Dumpster disinfectant, insecticide flavoring, cellulite peel. . . . We planned on and on, calculating fertilizer spreaders, railroad cars, and supertankers scattering secret seasoning to the ends of the earth!

Exhausted and pink with excitement, he presented me a four-ounce bottle of his miraculous concoction. It was Grandpa's recipe, he said reverently. He said he used it to flush his mules.

I wished him luck and bought half interest in the company for twelve dollars. Jim's Secret Seasoning . . . If you've got a secret, we've got the seasoning!

I've lived most of my life in places where it doesn't rain. The Texas Panhandle, southern New Mexico, the Imperial Valley, the high desert of Idaho, the front range of Colorado, and Chochise County, Arizona.

I don't take rain for granted.

FEAST OR FAMINE

In feast or famine, at least examine
the game we came to play
'Cause win or lose, it's how we use
the cards that come our way . . .

"Just let 'er rain," the rancher said. "We've built up quite a thirst.
I know the low road's plum washed out, the tank dam's bound to burst.
We'll have to plant the wheat again and clean the water gaps
But you won't hear this fool complain if it reaches to my chaps!

"The truth is, friends, we've needed this. We've been so dry so long
I thought I'd have to sell the cows and pay the piper's song.
The winter grass just lay there, stiff, for months it never changed.
I'd walk out through the cracklin' brown that covered all my range

"And watch the wind blow dust clouds where the good grass shoulda been.
I'd count the bales in the stack and calculate again.
The days of feedin' I had left before I'd have to face
The ultimate decision . . . what I'd do to save the place.

"The weatherman was helpful, 'cept he always told the truth!
  Piddlin' chance of ten percent meant it just rained in Duluth!
That's nice for Minnesota but it don't help me a bit,
  I gave up chewin' Red Man so I wouldn't have to spit!

"But he said last night 'a chance of rain.' More than just a trace.
  I washed the car and left the windows open just in case
And sure enough this mornin' big ol' clouds came rollin' in.
  They parked above the driveway and the thunder made a din

"That rattled all the winders in the house where I sat still.
  And at two it started rainin'. I still ain't got my fill.
It's comin' down in buckets like it's payin' back a debt.
  Me? I'm standin' in the front yard, in my shorts and soakin' wet!

"When the sun comes out tomorrow and sparkles all around
  Off pools and puddles standin' like big diamonds on the ground
I'll remember feast or famine, but when it comes to rain
  Ya take the feast when offered, if ya live out on the plain."

For some reason this commentary struck a chord. Even today the occasional NPR listener will mention it when we meet. And it is funny . . . unless it's yer cow.

LOOSE COW

One of the greatest feelings in the world is to see a cow loose on the road and realize it's not yours!

I know that sounds awful. And I do feel a little guilty sayin' it, but it's true. Of course, I do feel bad for whosever critter it is. And many's the time I've driven 'em down my lane and penned 'em up and called the owner of the wandering beast.

Chasin' somebody else's cow back where she belongs is kinda like drivin' a rented car. You do your best but you don't worry about the outcome quite as much. 'Specially if there's three or four neighbors helpin'!

Or passing motorists who are always willing to help. They're usually about as useful as a town dog, but they're enthusiastic! There's something that draws these Good Samaritans, like a car wreck or someone threatening to jump off a bridge.

If things are getting out of hand, there's always the possibility you can take down your rope and get a shot or two at her before she crawls through the fence.

'Course, if it's your cow, it's different. You're racin' around tryin' to get the lower pasture gate open whilst keepin' an eye on her last reported position. You're shouting orders at members of your family and the neighborhood pets, stationing motorists to slow down traffic and mostly makin' a fool of yourself.

The cow, on the other hand, has developed amnesia! She seems to have lost all memory of where she's been eating and sleeping for seven years. She's got her head up in the air like a drum major.

She's crashing through the neighbor's corn, headin' for the truck stop a mile away.

You manage to get her turned at the creek, where she breaks back south, in the opposite direction of your place. You are a'horseback and the wife's rattlin' down the end of the corn rows in the pickup. It's a good thing the thirty-thirty is with *her*!

The cow finally turns up the neighbor's drive and is converged on by six vehicles, swerving in like treasury agents at a moonshiners' convention.

You find her in the neighbor's shop calmly chewing on electrical wire.

With a little help you get her worked into his corral, then go back to your house and get the trailer and haul her home. An experience you won't long forget, 'specially since it will be the hot topic at the coffee shop for the next thirty days!

My youngest brother is one of the most talented men I know, and probably the smartest of us four—and he could pinch a penny. He's a real doctor now. We're proud of him. And yes, I still play on that old piano.

THRIFTY

Sharon had hauled the old piano home in a stock trailer. It came outta the Miner's Club in Mountain City, Nevada, where, according to the bartender, it had set since the early thirties. It was in sad shape, and one end of the ancient upright was full of holes. Bullet holes! Considering it had never been outta the bar, the piano player musta needed lessons.

Sharon gave the piano to me and I hauled it home, where it sat in my garage for a year.

Brother Steve came to visit. He's a talented musician with a craftsman's ability. He's also one of the thriftiest humans this side of Ebenezer Scrooge! He asked me if he could try to get the old piano in workin' order. "Of course!" I said. "I'll pay for the parts . . . whatever it takes!" I blocked out three or four hundred dollars in my mind. "Just save your receipts."

I came home that afternoon and the garage floor looked like an orchestra had exploded! He had dismantled that piano down to wire! The harp lay naked on the concrete.

Over the next several days I watched the rebuilding take place. Steve would go out on parts runs and return with a replacement hammer, just the right setscrew, or a used but serviceable piece of ivory. He took particular pleasure in makin' a shrewd trade. "Whatever it costs," I'd say, but he enjoyed finding a bargain.

One day he took me along on a parts run. We drove down the tracks, behind a big nursery, down a dusty road, and pulled up to a dilapidated house with a few outbuildings. I was struck by the fact that nothing was painted. There was one unspectacular sign that read PIANOS—TUNED AND FIXED.

We went inside and were greeted by the proprietor, who obviously knew Steve. He was a sad-lookin' man. The house was full of pianos. Even two in the kitchen. There was an empty can of tomato soup in the sink. I wandered through the rooms amongst the piano landscape, leaving Steve and the owner to do business.

From the looks of his home, he lived alone and probably not very high on the hog. Pianos in various stages of repair filled every available space.

I heard Steve and the man dickering in the kitchen.

"I'm sorry," Steve was saying, "I can't give more than five."

"I've got to get ten. It's surely worth ten," the old man pleaded.

I'm thinkin' to myself, "Steve, we can be generous. The ol' feller probably hasn't eaten in days. What's five bucks? Besides, I'm payin' for it!" But I knew better than to interfere. The bartering continued for several minutes. The old man finally came down to seven, but Steve wouldn't budge.

Finally, with a whimper, the old man gave in. He had met his match.

As we climbed into the pickup to leave I asked Steve what he had bought. He held up a little ribbon of red felt, maybe six inches long. "For the hammers," he explained.

I said, "Man, that don't look like it's worth five bucks!"

"Five dollars?" he said. "No, I gave five cents for it!"

The final bill for rebuilding my piano was $18.34.

GARTHED OUT!

Garth Brooks. Who? If you don't know, it's time you had a talk with your teenager. He is the biggest singing star in America today. Not just the biggest country music star, the biggest . . . period. Bigger than Michael Jackson, Bruce Springsteen, or any heavy metal, folk singin', rock and roll, rhythm and blues, classical, jazz, pop, New Age singin' star you wanna name!

I like country music. In my day it was Hank Thompson, Webb Pierce, Faron Young, and Lefty Frizzell. But they were never serious competition for Elvis or the Beatles.

But Garth Brooks is the beneficiary of a change in taste of America's fickle youth. I have no explanation why, but it happened. Two years ago my daughter was dreamy over mall music. Sort of a semisolid margarine rock and roll. Now she and her friends are buyin' Chris LeDoux, Reba, Clint Black, and Garth Brooks tapes. They are Garthed out to the max.

I'm glad. Matter of fact, I love it! I am still not discerning enough to tell all the new country singers apart, but, by gosh, now at least my kid and I both listen to the same cassettes.

She and I went to a Garth Brooks show recently. The closest I've ever been to that kind of concert was the Indianapolis 500. Between the spectacular light show and the screaming teenagers it was like a cross between Cape Canaveral and castrating pigs in a metal building.

Garth was masterful, and the crowd responded.

He thanked us for treating him like a real guy.

The very next evening I was tellin' cowboy stories to a crowd in the high school gym in Yukon, Oklahoma. The sign at the edge of town said "WELCOME TO YUKON, HOME OF GARTH BROOKS."

The folks gathered were just like my kinfolk. Just good country people. They were handling Garth's fame modestly, but you could tell they were proud that one of their own had gained such notoriety. I am, too. He dresses like us, knows how to wear a hat, plays pretty good guitar, and, even onstage, comes over as just a regular guy.

But the greatest accomplishment he and the new country music stars have made is to attract the fancy of our children. He gave us a little common ground.

Thanks, Garth, and thanks, Yukon.

Flint and I have discussed what Native Americans should be called if they choose not to be called Indians. He pointed out America was named after an Italian. I asked what term they used among themselves. He said, "Skins."

I think I'll wait till they decide.

P.S. Bailey White wrote that she liked this one. I wish she had called so I could have heard her voice.

PART INDIAN

Cutter said to me, "I'm part Indian."

I've heard that statement so many times from gringos that I've concluded I'm probably the only white man in North America who doesn't claim to be part Indian!

But when you think about it, what Cutter said is a pretty positive comment on the improving race relations in our country. White men in the early part of this century did not brag about being part Indian. It also appears that Indians are having a renewed sense of ethnic pride. That's a good thing.

I can understand their indignation regarding Columbus Day, although I'm not in favor of changing it. The battle's over. Columbus won. And I question their objection to professional sports team names like the Cleveland Indians, the Atlanta Braves, and the Cincinnati Redlegs. Personally, I think it's silly. But, I guess there's a pen rider somewhere who takes offense at the naming of the Dallas Cowboys. I do believe Indians are entitled to the extras they receive in their reservation treaties, like fishing rights and tax breaks.

Most of the Indians that I know personally are cowboys. Just regular people with families and horse trailers, jobs, and a little cow savvy. They live in places like Farmington, Winner, Fort Belknap, or Pawhuska. They go to rodeos, haul hay, attend high school basketball games, vote, go to church, shop at Wal-Mart, and saw *Dances with Wolves*.

Yet most urban citizens have little contact with reservation Indians. Therefore they depend on childhood Hollywood memories and the stereotypes created. Sometimes we embarrass ourselves.

Flint is a Scottsdale Comanche. He looks like heads on a buffalo nickel. He dresses regularly in elaborate Indian regalia. His job, he says, is to look good. And he sure does!

So he attracts attention like a peacock in a patch of sandhill cranes. He tells the story of a tourist who spotted him in a restaurant and asked him to pose for a photograph with his wife and kids. Flint obliged. The man took the picture, then left without introducing himself or asking Flint's name. Flint caught him and asked if he could take a picture of him and his family. The tourist was suspicious. "You don't even know me," he said. "Why do you want my picture?"

Flint said, "Well, you don't know me. Why did you want a photo of me?"

"You're an Indian," replied the tourist as if that explained everything.

Flint told the baffled tourist that in his house he had pictures of family and friends hangin' all over, but they were all Indians. He wanted a picture of at least one white man hangin' on the wall!

I used to ride bulls. . . . till my brains came in. Now I team rope. I've always loved rodeo.

WHITE OAKS RODEO

The Fourth of July weekend means different things to different people. Each of us may have a special memory of some Fourth of July. Maybe it's when you got married or had a baby or took that vacation to Yellowstone. To a lot of folks in the livestock business it means *rodeo*.

The Independence Day that stands out in my mind was many years ago. The big rodeo at White Oaks, New Mexico. You probably won't find White Oaks in your Rand McNally since it's a ghost town, but it's down around Carrizozo and Capitan, north of the Mescalero Indian reservation. It wasn't exactly a card-carryin' PRCA show, so it was right down my alley.

Two pardners and I arrived the mornin' of the Fourth in a fish-drownin', hat-soakin', slicker-testin' downpour! We entered up without looking at the stock. Just then the arena director came up the draw on a four-wheel-drive bay gelding drivin' the bucking stock. There were mares and colts, range ready, and to say they were thin would be kind. The bull ridin' turned out to be cow ridin' (they also doubled as doggin' stock).

The facilities were not quite National Finals approved. The arena was two football fields long and fenced in by sheep wire and cedar posts. The chute gate was made out of airport landing and baling wired to a railroad tie. Airport landing, for those of you who weren't in the Seabees, is a sheet of corrugated steel, six foot by eight foot and dotted with grapefruit-size holes. Each sheet weighs about three hundred pounds.

By the time the tape deck played "Barebackers Get Ready," the arena was a five-buckle-deep quagmire!

This was to be Conrad's first bareback ride. We got the riggin' down on the fightin' mare and I lent him my spurs. We kept whispering instructions and encouraging words. He rared back, pointed his toes, and nodded his head. The four men on the airport landing grunted it open about eighteen inches, where it stuck! The mare bolted to the daylight. Con's first voluntary leg movement, ended by lodging his left spur in a hole in the corrugated steel sheet. He had one hand in the riggin' and one foot stuck fast to the chute gate. He bravely hung on until he was twenty feet long. Then he lost his grip and dangled, head down, from the gate, his hat cutting a furrow in the mud as he swung back and forth like a pendulum.

"All that cowboy gets is your applause!"

My turn came and they lowered me down on the mustang's back. It was like straddling a two-by-eight. I called for the pony. We escaped the chute but she never bucked! She broke into a dead run and covered the two hundred yards like the starship *Enterprise*! It was beginnin' to look like she might not slow down. I bailed out just before she cleared the arena fence and lit out for parts unknown.

By the end of the rodeo I looked like a dyin' duck in a thunderstorm. Con's ankle was the size of his head, and the chute was in pieces. We were lucky, though; I heard later a feller broke his leg and one of the doggers was never found!

I admit to being uncomfortable with religious irreverence, although I am definitely a practitioner (of irreverence, I mean). Yet I know that each culture adapts objects of worship to a form its members can relate to.

This cowboy version of Christ's birth is from the dad's point of view. It is one of the most requested pieces of mine ever to run on NPR. It is one of two ("Rudolph's Night Off" is the other) to be repeated on purpose.

And I'll tell ya what, it can still give me goose bumps.

JOE AND MARIA
THE FIRST CHRISTMAS . . .
COWBOY STYLE

Now, I 'spect most of you cowboys have heard the story 'bout Christmas. How it came to be an' all, but I wanna 'splain it so y'all kin understand.

It started with this cowboy named Joe. He'd married a girl named Maria. Times was hard in them days. They's down to the crumbly jerky and one ol' paint gelding named Duke. To top it off, Maria was in the family way.

They'd been ridin' several days, with Joe mostly walkin'. They camped on the trail, and Maria was gettin' tired an' ornery. Late one night, December twenty-fourth, I think, they spotted the lights of a little burg. It was a welcome sight 'cause the weather'd turned coolish.

There was only one hotel in town, and Joe offered to chop wood or wash dishes for a room, but they were full up. The clerk said they could lay out their rolls in the livery stable. Git 'em outta the wind, anyway.

So Joe built 'em a nest in one of the stalls and went out to rustle

up some grub. When he came back, Maria was fixin' to have that baby. Well, Joe panicked.

He laid out his slicker, fluffed up the straw, and ran down the street lookin' for a doc. By the time he got back Maria'd done had that baby. It was a boy. She had him wiped off an' wrapped up in Joe's extra long john shirt.

Joe was proud, and Maria was already talkin' baby talk to the little one. They discussed what to call him. Joe wouldn't have minded if they'd named him Joe Jr., but Maria wanted to call him Jesus. A promise she'd made before Joe knew her.

Maria was tuckered. Jesus was sleepin' like a baby, and Joe was tickin' like a two-dollar watch. Fatherhood had hit him like a bag of loose salt! Just then he heard singin'.

In through the door of the livery come six Mexican sheepherders. They gathered around the baby and said he sure looked good. *"Niño especial,"* they said. Then they laid out some tortillas and commenced to visit.

Suddenly three fellas rode right into the livery. There was two Indian braves and a black cavalry scout. They told Joe that they'd had a vision and followed a star right to this very spot.

Joe said, "No kiddin'?"

"Shore nuf," they said. This was a special baby. He'd be a chief someday. This was good news to Joe. Not only that, they'd brought three buffalo hides, two handmade blankets, and a little poke of gold dust, which they gave to Joe to use for the baby.

Joe and Maria were overwhelmed. One of the herders tied together a little crib. He packed the bottom with straw and laid a sheepskin over it. Maria laid baby Jesus in it, and He never woke up, just gurgled and smiled.

Then the whole bunch of 'em stayed up all night talkin' 'bout Christmas.

Joe never forgot. He did his best to raise his son right, and when Jesus went on to bigger and better things, Joe'd remember that night. When a handful of strangers helped his little family through a hard time.

He told Jesus 'bout it when He was old enough to understand. How just a little kindness to yer fellowman can go a long way. Jesus took it to heart.

This poem stimulated several calls from ad agencies and car dealers around the country. However, on closer inspection, good judgment intervened when it dawned on them that they sold tropical fish.

After it ran on Morning Edition, *I thought it might be fun to send it to Tom and Ray . . . the car guys on NPR. I called one of the* Morning Edition *producers to see if they'd mind. "Yes," was her reply. "We do mind. We are very protective of our ornaments."*

MY KINDA TRUCK

I like a pickup that looks like a truck
        And not like a tropical fish.
Or a two-ton poodle with running lights
        Or a mutant frog on a leash.

Give me one tough as a cast-iron skillet
        With a bumper that's extra large
And a hood that weighs over eighty-five pounds
        And looks like the prow on a barge.

I like style but since when should a truck
        Be touted for comfort and ride.
Power windows on pickups? Reminds me of jeans
        With a zipper that zips up the side.

They should soak up the dents of everyday life
        Like a boxer losin' his teeth.
And I like a truck, when you lift up the hood
        You can see the ground underneath!

Pickups are kinda like welding gloves.
　　The pockmarks are part of the deal.
Not pretty, just built to get the job done.
　　Like the dummy behind the wheel.

Don't get me wrong, I know beauty's skin deep
　　And ugly is in the eye,
But to find out if your truck is my kinda truck
　　Here's a test that you can apply:

If you have a small wreck in the parking lot
　　By backin' a little too far,
Your only worry is how big a mess
　　You made of the other guy's car!

Another "true story" that seemed to stick in listeners' minds.

VERN'S WRECK

Vern thought he was gettin' by the Arctic cold snap pretty well. He owed his good fortune to preplanning, good equipment, good help, and a heated shop big enough to hold his feed trucks and front-end loader. They were havin' water tank problems in the pens, but who wouldn't at thirty-two below!

They kept the cattle fed. Vern waited out the dangerous weather with the uneasy feeling instinctive in all feedlot managers. I figger they are born reaching for a cigarette, a phone, and a bottle of Maalox!

"Boss, the faucet won't work in the ladies' bathroom."

"Simple," he thought, "bad washer, stripped handle, temporary aberration in the earth's magnetic field, a manatee plugging the pump . . . There are a lot of possibilities to explain a sudden lack of water into the office besides *frozen pipes!*"

But, of course, he was wrong.

Eventually they restored the water pressure only to find that the septic tank line was also frozen. Any manager will tell you that the average feedlot secretary can virtually live on diet pop and gossip, but will draw the line when forced to go to the bathroom outside, even when it's warm.

Vern inspected the ominous-looking septic tank cover. It was concrete, two and a half feet across, four inches thick, 150 pounds, and sealed in place with road rock and ice. It rested at the bottom of a frozen hole two feet deep.

He started chipping away at the edge with an ice pick. Then a kitchen knife, screwdriver, hatchet, crowbar, pickax, air hammer, backhoe, and front-end loader! He got a chain through the handle and hooked it to the loader bucket. Jim pulled up while Vern heated the seam with an acetylene torch. No luck.

With the grim determination of a two-year-old trying to eat Jell-O with his fingers, Vern poured two gallons of gasoline into the hole above the lid and lit it.

When the fire died he got a crowbar under the lip and pried up. It gave. Just as he heard the seal pop he remembered thinking, "I should have waited till that last little bit of fire went out . . ."

Whoosh! A sheet of flame took off Vern's left eyebrow and curled his earmuffs!

The lid slammed shut and transferred the pressure to the septic lines leading to the office.

Inside, the brand inspector, unaware of the plumbing problem, slipped into the rest room while the office staff was watching Vern's pyrotechnic display.

They said the damage to the bathroom was slight. Just a small circular indentation in the ceiling drywall just above the john. Size $7\frac{1}{4}$.

I have hay fever. I snort and sneeze, scratch my throat and rub my eyes. People who don't have allergies have difficulty understanding the misery: "Can't you stop that snorting and sniffling? It's drivin' me crazy!"

I'm genetically thin in spite of unusual eating habits—usually one meal a day, lots of red meat and candy. My idea of a salad is a jalapeño and Miracle Whip. There was a time I once considered fat people just lacking self-discipline. I now realize if you gain weight easily it is a constant battle to keep from gettin' fat. It is no less a burden than my hay fever.

Pencil predators prey on pinguescience and plumposity. Diet book authors are predatory pied pipers promising pulchritude while pilfering your pocket. Pshew . . . pardon me.

THE COWBOY AND HIS TAPEWORM

The world is on a diet. Seems no matter where you look
    Every fruitcake with a recipe has got a diet book.
But I think if they were honest, I'll bet they'd all concede
    The omniverous indifference of a cowboy's all you need.

He's in tune with Mother Nature and can live off of the land
    From the mountains of Montana to the muddy Rio Grande.
He's the ultimate consumer, he'll eat anything he finds,
    I've seen 'em lick the peelin' paint off Forest Service signs.

Or chew a steel fence post just to get down to the meat.
    He'll eat playin' cards and bob wire; anything a cow would eat,
A drumstick from a buzzard, a wilted Christmas wreath
    Then finish with a porcupine just to pick his teeth.

He'll drink water from a cow track, eat the claws of grizzly bear
  And you won't find no leftovers, he eats feathers, bone, and hair.
He makes hunters run for cover, he scares hikers half to death
  And he leaves no trace behind him, just the smell of his bad breath.

If you doubt what I have told you, I assure you that it's right,
  I have painted you a picture of a cowboy's appetite.
Though it may not look too pretty, it's exactly like I've drawn it.
  He'd prob'ly eat a bale of hay if you put whiskey on it.

So the world keeps on a'joggin' and a'sippin' diet pop
  But the cowboy and his tapeworm ride the range and eat nonstop.
If yer overweight and worried you should dine with him a while,
  'Cause there ain't no chubby cowboys in existence, in the wild.

Although I often see the funny side of things, I derive a great deal of soul sustaining satisfaction raising livestock. Calving time is where it all begins.

BENTLEY THE BORN-AGAIN BULL

It was one of those two o'clock mornin' calls: "Looked like everything was comin' jes' fine, Doc, then he got stuck! Could you come?"

On the way out to the ranch I put the truck on autopilot while my foggy brain sifted through the possibilities. Hip lock, more than likely, I figgered. I walked into the calvin' barn, shook the snow off my coat, and surveyed the scene. Fairly peaceful. Two unshaven cowboys playin' cards in front of the space heater and a good-sized heifer standing in the chute looking no worse for the wear. "Good," I thought, "the boys haven't worn the heifer out before they called." Or themselves either, for that matter.

I peeled down to my short-sleeve coveralls and went to survey the battlefield. There, underneath the heifer's cocked tail, peering out at the new world, was Bentley, the baby bull calf. All I could see was his head. With Mama's help he'd gotten far enough to pop his nose and his ears out and no farther. He didn't seem in distress, just a little embarrassed. He looked like some trophy hunter's prize hangin' on the den wall.

Since the umbilical cord hadn't broken yet he had no need to breathe, but he was lookin' around like a kid in a neck brace at the county fair. After my examination I concluded he had one front leg into the birth canal and the other pointing straight back. He was wedged in tight as a new hatband.

"Bentley," I said, "I hope you brought your scuba gear, because you've got to go back inside." I gave the heifer an epidural injection so she couldn't strain. I put my hand over his nose and started to push. Bentley raised an eyebrow and looked up at me. "You sure you've got a license to do this?" he said. "Sure," says I, "I bought it from a guy in Iowa when he sold out his practice."

It wasn't easy, but I popped the little duffer back in, straightened his legs, and then pulled him into the outside world.

He was typically ungrateful as I rubbed him down and pointed him to the breakfast nook under Mama's flank. He turned once and looked at me. "I've heard of being born again," he said, "but this is ridiculous!"

*This is pretty much a true story. Dan and Mary are lifetime friends,
and Roy Houck was one of the biggest buffalo raisers in the country.
You'll see his name in the credits of* Dances with Wolves. *He was a
grand gentleman but a country boy and never considered his contri-
bution would be less than enthusiastically received. He died in 1992
at the age of eighty-seven.*

BUFFALO TRACKS

As the typical cowman I've always been ambivalent about
buffalo. I'd hate to see them become extinct, but I've never
had a burning desire to have a bunch in the field between
my house and road.

I've handled them a little and I've observed they can be stubborn. Sort of like trying to work a landslide. But buffalo raisers
can become fanatics about their chosen species. They proffer several claims like low-cholesterol, low-fat meat, and they are high on
tradition.

I stayed one summer with Dan and Mary in Arizona. He built
his house over a period of years and it looks like the Taj Mahal
redecorated by Buffalo Bill. One of the features of which he is
most proud is his collection of trophy heads hanging from the
walls. I noticed that he had no buffalo skull. He had been such a
gracious host, I vowed to remedy that deficiency. When I got home
I called Roy, who raises buffalo in South Dakota. I asked him to
send my friend in Arizona a buffalo skull. I received the bill two
weeks later and sat back to wait for an effusive thank-you card. It
never came.

The following summer I went to see Dan and Mary. The buffalo
skull was nowhere in sight. We sat around drinking coffee and I
waited for them to mention my gift. Finally I joked that what this

house really needed was a buffalo skull. Mary turned on me like a bitin' dog! *"It was you!"* she accused!

Turns out that in that previous August, the post office had called and notified Mary of a pickup. They sounded urgent. It was four miles to the P.O., so she stopped by next morning on her way to work. The nervous mailmen hastily loaded a three-foot-by-three-foot heavy wooden crate into the back of her hatchback. Stenciled across the crate were the letters **S-K-U-L.** Mary noted a peculiar odor. It was not entirely pleasant.

She drove thirty-two miles into Phoenix, parked and locked her car, and went into work. The temperature that afternoon by the bank clock was 109 degrees! By 5:30 P.M. a crowd had gathered in the parking lot to watch flies write "HELP ME" on the inside of her steamy windshield!

Mary drove home with the windows down and the hatchback up, covering her nose with her Peter Pan collar and gagging into her Pierre Cardin shirtsleeve!

Screeching to a halt in front of the Taj Mahal, this fashionably attired, stench-crazed woman clawed and tumbled the sixty-pound crate out of her car. It tore her left stocking and dripped black fluid on her ivory-colored Dior imitation silk dress and open-toed Gucci pumps. She grabbed a greasy tire iron from Dan's pickup and pried a board off the top. Peering up at her, with a blank look, was an eye!

I've never asked ol' Roy why he didn't skin the head. 'Course, I've never admitted to Mary that it was me who had sent it either. Sometimes it's best to let sleeping dogs lie!

If you knew Sam, you would realize this story is not as far-fetched as it sounds. He makes good brisket and cabbage salad and has the biggest butterfly collection I've ever seen.

THE GREAT CHICKEN RUN

Because of my peculiar qualifications I am asked to assist in some unconventional projects. Recently I served as a consultant on a semipro all-natural heavyweight chicken run.

Sam raises chickens. Not in a big way, but chickens are like CDs or cassettes; if yer gonna have one, you might as well have a bunch. Yet, old chickens present a problem. They cannot be retired gracefully. You might turn an old faithful horse out to pasture or stuff yer best bird dog, but a chicken, even in her twilight years, engenders very little loyalty or respect. Sam had a surplus of blue-haired layers that had lost their bloom.

A quick call to the local sale barn revealed that they had discontinued their Thursday afternoon chronic feeder chicken sale. Mr. Campbell (of noodle soup fame) and Mr. McNugget bought old hens, but only by the train carload. By a fortuitous conversation with a neighbor, Sam discovered that first-generation immigrants from Vietnam and other Southeast Asian countries prized the meat of mature chickens.

Armed with this information, Sam applied for a peddler's license. It was necessary for him to post a thousand-dollar bond, in cash, to ensure that the city collected its sales tax, which is not charged on live chickens anyway. No matter; Sam said it sorta took the free outta free enterprise.

Saturday morning we gathered all the old chickens in the neighborhood, plus a few grasshopper ducks, and loaded them in the back of his Toyota pickup. Down the road we went with our convoy of foundering feathered fossils trailing duck down and chicken fluff like a cattail in the hands of a three-year-old. We pulled into the parking lot of Mai Van's Oriental Grocery and Unusual Seafood.

We announced that we had live chickens for sale. Word spread like cheap wine on a white tuxedo. We were surrounded! Sam was dickerin' chickens, duckerin' ducks, peddlin' pullets, and purveyin' poultry! I was the broiler bagman, tyin' their scaly paws together as fast as Sam could catch 'em. One nice gentleman asked if we had any merganser ducks. I told 'im all we had was what we could catch at City Park. He laughed, then asked about my dog. I changed the subject.

An attractive mother of three asked, through her six-year-old son, "How much for these five chickens?" Sam was naturally sympathetic for the young woman, trying to raise her family in a foreign land. He proffered seven dollars for all five. She countered with six dollars and a tear. Sam settled for five bucks. Could we help her load them? she asked. Certainly, we said. We put a cardboard box with five live chickens in the trunk of her Lincoln Continental.

We sold thirty-eight chickens, two roosters, and six ducks; grossed eighty-three dollars; learned how to say "live chicken" in Vietnamese, Mong, Cambodian, and Laotian; had a great time; and fostered goodwill between two very different cultures. Not bad for a day's wok.

Dar la vuelta. *To give a turn. The Mexican roping term passed on to gringos who bastardized it to "dally." After roping a bovine, the tail of the rope still in your hand is wrapped once around the saddle horn and held. "Dally'ed," as it were. Some think it is safer than bein' tied "hard and fast" to the saddle horn. But dallying has its dangers. Should you accidentally get a thumb or finger between the rope and the horn . . . well . . . that's what this commentary is about.*

DISAPPEARING DIGITS

When Winston Churchill and Richard Nixon made the victory sign, you probably thought the same thing I did . . . Them boys ain't team ropers!

Come to think of it, I've never seen a roper point at the TV camera and say, "We're number one!"

Ropers are at a definite disadvantage hitchhiking, buttoning a shirt, and eating with chopsticks.

Many a roper has fished a finger out of his glove as a result of a slipshod dally. It always gives me a queasy feeling to see some roper on his hands and knees searching through the arena dirt like he was lookin' for a contact lens.

In any group of ropers you're liable to find a sampling of fellers who can't count to ten. Most take it in good stride and don't dwell on the handicap of missing a digit or two. It's the price you pay. As they say, "If you ain't been bucked off, cowboy, then you ain't been on many!"

I've still got all my fingers and thumbs, so bein' a sorry roper has its advantages. You gotta catch 'em to lose 'em!

Losing a finger or thumb in the dally is no laughing matter. It's a lot more permanent than getting a haircut. Modern medicine and skilled surgeons can often replace the severed phalange. Of course, the success of the operation depends on the condition of the missing piece and whether or not you can find it.

Young John walked into the emergency room with his hand wrapped in a towel.

"What happened?" the doctor asked.

"We were brandin' at the Pocket. I roped a calf and hung my thumb in the dally."

"Well, let me see the piece you cut off," said the doc.

"I didn't bring it."

"Do you know where it is? If it's in good shape we might be able to save it."

"Yeah, I do. But when it popped off, it sailed out over my horse's head pretty as you please. My good dog jumped up and snagged it in midair!"

"Great scott, son! Whyn't you shoot the dog?"

"Shoot the dog? He's the best one we got!"

I have the pleasure of knowing the kind of people that John Wayne tried to portray on the screen. Harry Johnson was one of these people. When he retired from our outfit it didn't set well with him. He'd come out to the brandin's and cow workin's but he wouldn't help. All he did was sit around and talk with the cook. I think he felt useless. To me, when he retired from a lifetime a'horseback he just put on his bedslippers and waited to die.

Lookin' Back

Harry was a cowboy all his life. I don't mean no pickup-drivin', two-way-radio-talkin', Marlboro-smokin', team-ropin', bee-boppin', baseball cap cowboy . . . I mean a real cowboy.

All my life I been eatin' trail dust, punchin' cows and sleepin' in a bedroll.

I washed my socks in the river a million times and stunk so bad I smelled like an old beaver hide.

My feet's been froze and my head's been baked; I've growed enough hide over rope burns to cover ten saddles.

There's been times in my life I'd have give every dime I had for a dry boot.

I guess I've rode three or four hundred horses into the ground; some good, some not so good.

I've knowed an equal number of men; some good. But I thank whatever God watches over me that I've known at least one good woman.

I've probably lost more spurs, wore out more ropes, drunk more bad coffee and more good whiskey than most men.

I've eat them damn beans and chewed that tough meat till Hell wouldn't have it.

I been hungry and tired, cold and broke, and there's been times I was ten miles from camp dyin' for a smoke and not a match in my pocket.

But I've been happy. Lord, that sun comin' up over the edge of the canyon, the chill comin' off the sage, that first cup of coffee 'fore you saddle up,

You couldn't buy that from me with fancy cars or easy chairs or Ph.D.s.

This earth's give me a fair shake so far, but I don't see many young fellers followin' my footsteps.

But, by God, if some green buckaroo wants to make a hand someday I say more power to him.

I left him an easy trail to follow.

Another popular commentary. I think it must be the last line.

POLITICAL CORRECTNESS

It's coming! Political Correctness in the Animal Kingdom! I have conferred with those fervent homogenizers of the once-colorful and descriptive English language to formulate the following list:

Stray dog: Both words are unacceptable. They imply that a four-legged mongrel is subsisting as a vagrant. We have chosen the term Misdirected Wagamorph.

Mustang: Definitely out! Associated too much with a greedy automotive corporation. We are going to protect them into extinction. They shall henceforth be called Adoptable Equine Derivatives.

Killer whales: Need I say more? The name suggests that these beautiful creatures would rather kill and eat living things than down a kelp burger in the shape of a baby seal. We're calling them the Masked Cetacea.

Fat steers: Entirely out. No slur shall be made about their weight or their sexual predicament. Each cattle buyer will now deal in Ready Edibles. No, that won't work either, can't mention bulls. How 'bout Ripened Ruminants?

Quarter horse: No chance. The hypersensitive could interpret that to mean he's three-quarters something else. I've coined the term Dollar Horse.

Polled Hereford: Come on, now! Wouldn't it be less discriminatory to rename them the Unhorned Himherford?

Too many of our creatures were named by that original chauvinist, Adam, with unconscious patronizing to sex, gender, race, religion, size, handicap, mental state, congenital deformity, or odd behavior.

Consider how insensitive we are to call something a nanny goat, a laying hen, a preying mantis, a peafowl, a woodpecker, a short-nosed sucker, or a turkey.

I admit I've been called a turkey, but I thought it was a step up from a dodo.

But if we are truly worried about the Political Correctness fad, what are we gonna call a cowboy? A Two-Legged Ungulate Overperson? Why not?

"Git along, little Disenfranchised Mobile Nurture Seeker."

There are places on earth where you realize man's presence is only temporary. I wrote this on Oregon State Highway 395, between Wagontire and Lakeview.

THE BIG HIGH AND LONESOME

The big high and lonesome's a place in my mind
  like out from Lakeview to Burns.
Or up on the Judith or at Promontory
  'bout where the UP track turns.
It's anywhere you feel tiny
  when you get a good look at the sky
And sometimes when it's a'stormin'
  you can look the Lord in the eye.

I stood and watched in amazement
  out on San Augustine Plain
While the sky turned as black as the curtains in Hell
  and the wind come a'chasin' the rain.
And standing there watching I felt it
  in the minutes before it arrived
An unearthly stillness prickled my skin
  like the storm itself was alive.

When it hit, it hit with a fury
  the wind with its saber unsheathed
Led the charge with the scream of a demon;
  the storm was barin' its teeth.
The thunder cracked and the sky split apart
  with a horrible deafening roar
I felt like a fox in a cage made of bones
  in sight of the hounds at the door.

The blackness shook like a she-bear.
The lightning blinded the sun
The rain fell like bullets around me
scattering dust like a gun!
It was over as quick as it started
leaving it peaceful instead
The only sound was the beat of my heart
pounding inside of my head.

I took off my hat, too shaken to move
afraid of making a sound
I felt like a man on the head of a pin
with nobody else around.
But the sun was already sparkling
in raindrops still wet on my face.
The big high and lonesome is only God's way
of putting a man in his place.

Another true story

LANDSCAPING

Genie noticed the bottle of Jack Daniel's on the kitchen table when she got home late that night. Like most lettuce farmers, if she kept whiskey in the house, it was not usually kept on the kitchen table.

She marched into the bedroom to find her husband, Don, sprawled out on the bed with one pant leg off and one sock on. He looked like a body that had been dragged off the bottom of a lake.

He began shakily, "I was watchin' TV in my shorts when I heard a ruckus on the lawn . . . and mooing."

Don went to the window and peeked out to discover his front yard covered with cows! They were obviously from neighbor Willie's dairy across the road. It was a surreal picture under the yard light: black and white Holstein clowds on a sky of green grass.

Don ran out on the porch waving and shouting at the curious beasts. Although the cows paid him little mind, Willie's bull developed an immediate urge to mash Don to a pulp. Don did a wheelie on the cement walk and ran back into the house. The bull mounted the porch steps and charged the door! After ramming it several times he clattered through the lawn furniture and mowed down a good-sized decorative evergreen.

Don waited a few minutes, put on his jeans, and nervously eased out, intending to shoosh the cows off the lawn, which was now covered with deep tracks and cow patties. It was just as he stepped on a leaking sprinkler head with his socks on that the bull charged from behind the arborvitae.

He raced to the front door, clearing the jamb and slamming it in the bull's face. He could see the paint cracking as the bull pounded on the other side. The bull then crashed off the porch and rammed the passenger side of his daughter's red Monte Carlo. Then he clammered back onto the porch to resume his lusty bawling and door demolition.

Don was hyperventilating as he tried to dial the sheriff.

"He's not here but I can call him on the radio," offered the receptionist. "What's the complaint?"

"Ma'am, yer not gonna believe this, but a cow's tryin' to break into my house!"

The sheriff had come and gone and the sirens had all died away by the time Genie got home. The front lawn looked like Dade County. As she listened to her pitiful exhausted husband unfold his bizarre tale, she was torn between the need to comfort and hold him and the uncontrollable desire to snort and fall over backwards in gales of hysterical laughter. She simply wiped her eyes and went to the kitchen and poured herself a shot.

IT AIN'T EASY BEIN' A COWBOY

It ain't easy bein' a cowboy
 like the Marlboro man
'Cause the public expects us
 to all be from Texas
And roll cigarettes with one hand.
  An' I don't even smoke!

Hollywood painted a picture
 they like to perpetuate.
The streets of Laredo
 still echo his credo
That a cowboy always shoots straight.
  An' I can't hit the broad side of a buffalo!

Then Nashville improved on the image
 so now a cowboy can be
an illegal alien
 like Willie and Waylien
Or a soap opera retiree.
  An' I can't even sing!

I envy that smooth urban cowboy
 whose dance card always seems full
I'd almost be willin'
 to take penicillin
Or ride the mechanical bull.
  'Cause I'm tired of kissin' my horse!

It's hard to compete with Casey Tibbs,
    Louie L'Amour and John Wayne
When the best that you've done
    is a buckle you won
Worn smooth since that youthful campaign.
    Now I can't read without glasses!

The twentieth-century cowboy,
    what I'm supposed to be;
That rare combination
    of civilization
And Jessie James on a spree.
    But like I said . . .

It ain't easy bein' a cowboy
    so I've made myself a vow
To avoid inspection
    and public rejection
I'll jes' stay out here . . . with the cows.
    Hell, if it was easy, I'd be somethin' else!

If God were going to set up a situation where someone could get hurt, He could start with a bipedal, erect creature with no claws or fangs, a predatory ego, and the judgment of an armadillo. Then He could add a thousand-pound critter with hooves, horns, a thick skull, and the foul disposition of a government receptionist. Third, He could include a twelve-hundred-pound animal that walks on its toes, can buck like a train wreck, and spooks at a fluttering newspaper.

Finally, to guarantee injury on a regular basis, He could connect them all with a forty-foot unbreakable nylon rope.

Thus was born . . .

THE OLD STOVE-UP COWBOYS OF AMERICA
CONSTITUTION AND BYLAWS

A FRATERNAL ORGANIZATION OF ACTIVE, SEMIACTIVE, AND RETIRED COWBOYS WHO CARRY PHYSICAL SCARS AS A PERMANENT SOUVENIR OF LIFE ON THE RANGE.

OUR NOBLE PURPOSE IS TO PROMOTE COMRADESHIP AMONG COWPOKES WHO SUSTAINED INJURY IN THE LINE OF DUTY; I.E., YEARS IN THE SADDLE, RODEO FRACTURES, DIGITS LOST IN DALLYS, BAR FIGHTS, LOOSE CINCHES, TIGHT BOOTS, AND DOG BITES.

AND TO RECOGNIZE THOSE COWBOYS WHO HAVE SUFFERED AS A RESULT OF LIGHTNING STRIKE, BROKEN ROPES, BAD HORSES, SNAKE BITES, HANDYMAN JACKS, PRICKLY PEAR, FENCE STRETCHERS, RINGY HEIFERS, BARB WIRE, GATES OF ALL KINDS, AND PRAIRIE DOG TOWNS.

BE IT KNOWN THAT WHEREAS IT IS READILY ADMITTED, CONCEDED, AND GRANTED THAT LIFE AS A COWBOY CAN BE DANGEROUS

AND WHEREAS MOST COWBOYS PERSIST IN THEIR OCCUPATION UNAWARE, OR UNMINDFUL, OF THE HAZARDS PECULIAR TO THEIR PROFESSION

AND WHEREAS IT IS UNLIKELY THAT MODERN TECHNOL-OGY WILL EVER REPLACE THE HORSE AND ROPE AS OFFENSIVE WEAPONS IN BOVINE WARFARE

AND WHEREAS NO PERSON OF SOUND MIND AND BODY WOULD TRADE PLACES WITH A COWPOKE, EVEN ON A BET

AND WHEREAS ACCIDENTS CAN HAPPEN TO EVEN THE MOST CAREFUL COWBOY

BE IT RESOLVED THAT THE <u>OLD STOVE-UP COW-BOYS OF AMERICA</u> WAS FORMED IN HONOR OF THESE KNIGHTS OF THE SADDLE AND BANDAGE.

PRESIDENT: *Kenny House,*
MARSHAL OF WESTERN KANSAS
DIRECTOR: *Ace Reid*
OTHER DIRECTOR: *Baxter Black*

For membership information submit a written description of yer injuries. Consideration will be given to location and cause. Visible scars or X rays should be available on request.

For Delilah's sake I changed her name in the story. But Rob is as real as Wrong-Way Corrigan.

THE GRAPEVINE

How better to impress his new lady friend, thought Rob, than to take her to his friend's rancho for an afternoon branding and barbecue.

She would be pleased to see that he had many friends who drove pickups with chrome grill guards, tinted windows, and coordinated paint jobs. He admitted to himself that his own outfit was less ostentatious. His '64 model two-horse trailer had been repaired so many times that it looked like a well-drillin' rig. The '76 pickup was using two quarts of oil to a tank of gas, and his horse was . . . well, ol' Yella looked right at home.

Rob was eager as a piddlin' puppy when he picked up Delilah and headed north outta the Los Angeles area. He was anxious to make a decent impression, but one large obstacle lay in the pit of his stomach like a pea in the Princess's mattress . . . The Grapevine! It was a monster of a hill dreaded by truckers and people who still drove a Chevy Nova.

The engine was screamin' and smokin' like a burnin' pile of creosote posts when they finally leveled out at the summit of the Grapevine. Rob had sweated through his shirt but he sighed with relief as he gave Delilah a comforting look. She smiled back uneasily. Then the motor blew! A big dent appeared in the hood, and it sounded like someone had dropped a Caterpillar track into the fan.

They coasted silently into a service station at the bottom of the grade. He assured his sweetheart there was *"no problema."* He had lots of friends nearby. Her reaction was one of forced optimism.

By dark he'd borrowed a pickup from Hank and they both agreed returning back home was the best option. He loaded Yella, hooked up the trailer, and back over the Grapevine they flew! Halfway down Rob managed to slip his arm behind Delilah's neck. Soon she was lulled into discussing her dreams of home and family. She snuggled closer as he watched a tire bounce by him on the driver's side. No headlights shone in his rearview, but he couldn't help but notice the huge rooster tail of sparks spraying up from beneath his trailer. He could see her astonishment in the flickering light.

Rob wheeled the screeching rig to the shoulder. Together they unwired the trailer doors and Yella stepped out, unhurt. Rob tied him to the highway fence and unhooked the trailer. Rob's facial tic had returned.

Seemingly in control, he jumped in the pickup and headed south for the nearest phone to borrow a trailer. He returned to the scene to find Yella grazing in the median with semis whizzing by on both sides and his date shivering over the still-warm axle, forgotten. She, herself, was smoldering. She spoke not a word and Rob conceded to himself that it was gonna be hard to regain her confidence.

In the space of twelve hours and fifty miles he had left his pickup, his trailer, his horse, and his girl scattered from one end of the Grapevine to the other.

Next day he towed the pickup to the shop. He left his trailer to be impounded by the State Police. His horse made it home safe, but Delilah changed her phone number, wrote him out of her will, and has not been heard of since!

You can't make this stuff up!

THE TRANQUILIZER GUN

Unless you're a tiger trimmer in Tanganyika, the tranquilizer gun has not lived up to its potential. During its preliminary promotion, it was touted as the greatest invention since the rope. But, in the livestock business, it has never quite fulfilled its expectations. The biggest problem seems to be its predictable unpredictable results.

Most large animal vets have tranquilizer guns. Some of my colleagues learned the fine art of using one. The rest of us have had it stuck away with our fleams and hog cholera vaccine since 1974. I suspect "operator error" had a lot to do with our failures.

Dr. Green said he and Dr. Corley used it with success when they were gatherin' wild cattle down in Mississippi. It gave them an advantage over the better ropers in the area.

Even a good roper has to get within throwin' distance.

The Outlaw family had eight cows and one uncatchable wanderin' bull. The bull was part braymer . . . the uncatchable part.

Mr. Outlaw kept 'em in a scrubby pasture next to his neighbor. This neighbor practiced rotational grazing and his pasture was lush.

Mr. Outlaw's bull spent most of his time at the neighbor's. Since the bull managed to crawl back through and breed the eight cows every spring, Mr. Outlaw saw no reason to be concerned.

When the threats became unbearable, Mr. Outlaw finally agreed to sell his wanderin' bull. He called on Drs. Green and Corley to expedite the matter.

Our boys arrived on the scene, chased the bull back onto the

Outlaw property and began to trail him through the brush. The bull took a breather in a clearin' and our ballistic vets pulled down and nailed him with the tranquilizer dart. They got him roped and staggered to the open-top trailer, where they tied him in. The bull laid down and passed out.

Mr. Outlaw was pleased: "I'm takin' him over to Bryan Brothers. Oughta git a pretty penny for him!"

"Yup," said Dr. Green. "But he'd be worth more if he walked outta the trailer, fer sure."

"You bet, Doc. How long you reckon it'll take this tranquilizer to wear off?"

"Forty-five minutes to an hour."

"Great! I better git goin'!"

That afternoon they saw Mr. Outlaw back home at the coffee shop.

"How'd it go?" they asked.

"Oh, fine, fine. Made a lotta money. Only had one problem. He was still down when I got there. I had to run him through the car wash twice to get him awake enough to sell!"

This describes a few of my friends. 'Course, they might say it is pretty autobiographical.

KEEPIN' BUSY

S kip, whattya doin' now'days?"

"Oh, I'm doin' a little day work for Irsik and ridin' two green colts for fifty dollars a month. I think I've just about sold that load of salvage lumber I traded Mr. Jolly out of.

"Some guy came by the other day and wants me to audition for the Marlboro man. Said they pay pretty good even if they don't pick me.

"I've put down on some lease pasture. If my pardner comes through we're gonna turn out a few steers.

"I've got some other deals workin', playin' guitar with Butch and Jim on Fridays at the Fort, shoein' the odd horse now and then. Ol' Man Gammon pays me to irrigate his yard every other Sunday.

"Other than that . . . not much."

Thank goodness his wife has a job. Skip is one of those fine fellers who eases through life from one project to another just fillin' in the gaps.

He's the man you can call at noon on Tuesday and get some help. Chances are he could hook up a trailer and go pick up something for you at the sale. 'Specially if you gassed him up first.

He's one of the few individuals who never misses a ropin', a weekday grade school track meet, a car wreck, a beer bust, a horse sale, a pancake feed, or a political rally.

He'd no more think of makin' a "career change" that would require movin' outta town than he'd consider filing his income tax on time.

He was offered a seasonal job with the highway department as a sign fluctuater but declined at the last minute 'cause somethin' came up.

I've always been curious what he writes on a form when it asks his occupation. Executive enabler? Implementation specialist? Relationship analyst? Impediment counselor? Maybe just Omniconsultant.

Every time I visit with him the list of what he's doin' changes. A few come off the top of the roll, some new ones are included at the bottom. But he's always gotta lotta irons in the fire.

He's the inspiration for that Ol' Coyote Cowboy proverb: "If it takes somebody more than ten minutes to tell you what they do for a livin', they're probably self-unemployed!"

This has always been one of the favorite poems I've written. It should be read aloud.

THE EPITAPH

That ol' man could sure set a post. Three foot down
    in the hardest ground, grunt and thud, chink and chime.
Bedrock trembled beneath his bar. Each new whack
    broke the back of granite old as time.

Be easier to move it. The hole, that is.
    But that wasn't his way of settin' a post.
His ran like a soldier's backbone, straight as a die
    to the naked eye. Perfect . . . not just close.

He'd scoop the dirt into it in a careful way.
    Like sculptor's clay he'd add an inch or two.
"Each one counts," *he'd say to me, then tamp that thing*
    till the bar would ring and the earth was black and blue.

He set cedar and steel but what he liked most
    was an eight-foot post, the butt of a telephone pole.
Called it "plantin' a deadman," . . . for bob wire fence
    to stretch against. Made a hell'uva hole!

Big enough to bury a dog. Speakin' of which,
    last week he pitched straight over facedown and died.
Not buildin' fence like you might think but on his knees
    tendin' trees that grew on the windbreak side.

For twenty years we neighbored well, which just makes sense,
    our common fence was always strong and tight.
But, Lord, he did things the hard way! Flat wore me out!
    But I don't doubt he tried to do 'em right!

They struggled for an epitaph to consecrate,
    in words ornate, the place they'd lay his head.
They didn't ask me. I weren't no kin to the lad
    but if they had, this is what I'd said,

"He could sure set a post." One man's stand
    in the shifting sand of the world as it is today
That offered hope. An anchor, dug in deep,
    that helped to keep us all from driftin' away.

This commentary caused a stir. It aired during the acrimonious debate of the Clinton administration's plan to nationalize health care. I was told that NPR headquarters received over 100 phone calls requesting copies on the morning it ran.

A FOX IN THE HENHOUSE

Things were bad in the barnyard. Especially in the chicken house.

It hadn't always been that way. Farmer Lopez used to know every hen by name. He raised them from chicks, rocked their eggs, and communed with them. He fed them faithfully, the best layer mash he could buy and lots of good clean water.

The hens reciprocated by layin' an egg a day. It was a good working relationship. If a hen skipped a day or Farmer Lopez was a little late with the feed, neither made a federal case out of it.

Then the demand for eggs went up. Farmer Lopez traded up from a screened-in chicken duplex to a giant poultry palace. He took in more hens. He still gave them feed and water, but since there were so many he wasn't able to give them the personal attention they had become use to. He hired a duck to oversee the mechanical feeder. He put the goat in charge of counting eggs.

The hens became disgruntled. They complained. Farmer Lopez wanted to go talk to them personally but he was busy meeting with the goat. So he hired another duck.

Lurking outside the chicken house was the fox. He had never been able to get near the hens when Farmer Lopez was doin' the feedin' and egg gatherin'. But now, every time the goat called a meeting or the ducks dozed off, Brother Fox would help himself.

Soon Farmer Lopez was forced to employ the mule as a security guard to protect the hens from the fox. But this required that they lay more eggs to pay the mule.

The fox stole the mule's eggs while he was guarding the hens. Then, when the mule took a break, the fox slipped into the hen-house and knocked off a hen. This resulted in less eggs and more meetings with the goat. Now and then, while the goat and Farmer Lopez were meeting, Mr. Fox would nail a duck. And if Farmer Lopez went to help the duck, the goat turned up missing.

Eventually, the Department of Barnyard Regulation (the DBR) became aware of the chaos in the chicken house.

"Something must be done!" pleaded the hens, Farmer Lopez, the mule, the three-legged goat, and the remaining duck.

"We'll form a secret committee to reorganize the chicken house," declared the DBR. "But we will not seek the opinions of Farmer Lopez, the hens, the mule, the duck, or the goat. They lack the revolutionary vision required. The committee will be com-posed exclusively of foxes!" pronounced the chairman of the DBR, a fox himself.

"National health care in the United States is a mess! We'll form a task force to solve the problem," declared the president, a lawyer himself.

This may be one of those "urban legends" that is told and retold in many versions and always preceded by "They say this really happened."

PARAKEETS AND DOGS

Most of us who deal with animals on a regular basis are familiar with the books of that well-loved veterinarian and author James Herriot. He seems to embody everybody's image of the kindly, competent country practitioner. Occasionally wrong but always well intentioned.

Vets are often called on to minister to the needs of the owner as well as the patient.

Dr. Herriot told one story that is a variation of a tale not unheard of by many veterinarians, regarding a blind woman's parakeet. The parakeet sat in his cage and sang. He was the old lady's sole companion.

Dr. Herriot was called to her house one day with the complaint that Perry wasn't eating. Doc withdrew Perry from his cage and reassured Missus that his beak was overgrown. He could fix it in a jiffy. Missus was so relieved. She loved Perry's singing so much. Doc carefully snipped the beak, and when he went to replace the bird in his cage, he made the startling discovery that Perry was dead as a crowbar.

The rest of the chapter involved Dr. Herriot's mad search to find a live replacement for Perry with the genuine intention of preventing the blind lady from suffering distress.

It doesn't just happen to vets. A pet shipping container arrived at the big-city airport. As it was wending its way through the bowels of the baggage facility, one of the employees peeked into Skipper's cage. She immediately removed the dog crate and called her supervisor. After some gentle nudging with a short stick they agreed that Skipper was stiff as a two-by-four and was, in fact, dead!

A crowd of baggage handlers gathered. They were terribly concerned. They were discussing who to blame when one of the men said his neighbor was feeding a stray that was the spitting image of Skipper! He was sent to get the dog at any cost while the supervisor went out front and stalled the passenger.

Within an hour they had switched collars, stuffed the stray into the carrier and Skipper in a sack.

"That's not my dog," said the disgruntled passenger.

"Well, sure it is, ma'am," asserted the supervisor.

"Nope. That's not Skipper."

"He came in this carrier checked from Des Moines. It says so right on the tag here."

"Not him!"

"Look! He's waggin' his tail! He's wearin' his collar! It's got to be your dog."

"Sure isn't," she said. "My dog's dead."

I grew up a Southern Baptist. We were staunch believers in Cre-
ationism. Then I went to veterinary school. There is an almost inces-
tuous relationship between scientists that demands "if you expect me
to believe you when you tell me my horse has navicular disease, then
I expect you to believe me when I tell you this rock is twenty-five mil-
lion years old." Scientists believe in evolution.

So I have spent a lifetime bearing the burden of trying to resolve
Genesis and evolution. This was my solution.

COWBOY TIME

If Genesis was right on track concerning Adam's birth
And seven days was all it took to build the planet Earth,
Then where does carbon dating fit? And all the dinosaurs?
Plus all that other ancient stuff that happened on our shores?

Now, I believe in scientists. They aren't just lunatics!
But I believe in Genesis, which leaves me in a fix,
The answer finally came to me while making up this rhyme.
God made the earth in seven days, but . . . that was Cowboy Time!

Have you ever called the shoer to set aside a day?
You scrutinize your calendar, say, "Tuesday'd be okay."
The big day comes, you take off work, alas, he's never seen.
You call him back and he inquires, "Which Tuesday did you
mean?"

Did you ever place an order to get a saddle made?
An A-fork tree with padded seat and silver hand-inlaid,
As decades pass, all you can do is sit around and eat
So by the time it finally comes you've padded your own seat!

A friend came by on July 4th. He swore he couldn't stay
But then he said, "For just a bit." He left on Christmas Day!
"A couple days," "a little while," "not long," or "right away!"
Should not be taken lit'rally in cowboyville today.

But like I said, the precedent was set so long ago.
The angels had to learn themselves what all good cowboys know.
They worried if they didn't work to keep the schedule tight
That Earth would not be finished by the deadline Sunday night.

They'd never learned to think in terms of rollin' with the flow
But God does things on Cowboy Time . . . to watch the flowers grow.
He bade the angels to relax and said, "For Heaven's sakes,
I'll get it done in seven days . . . however long it takes!"

The flood in the heartland in spring and summer '93 changed a lot of lives. It was one thing to hear or see sporadic updates while looking from my semiarid place here in the West. But to be in the midst of this "act of God" every day for weeks and months on end had to engender blind faith, hopelessness, or insanity.

When I recorded this for NPR I asked friends of mine to read the quoted parts, and yes, my preacher (a good Congregationalist) orated Genesis. . . .

THE FLOOD

It's just the mud. The continuing aftermath of month after month of unending, unrelenting, boot-suckin', calf-drownin', ground-killin', mind-numbin', heart-soakin', head-bangin', sky-watchin', depressing, debilitating, backbreaking, bullying rain.

"Don't know why, ain't no sun up in the sky . . . stormy weather . . ."

Even if you got your corn planted late, it still takes a lotta sun. Corn needs so many "heat increments" to make it mature. Too muddy to plant, too cool to grow. A right cross and a left hook. This one-two punch K.O.'d a lot of farmers in Iowa, Illinois, Minnesota, Wisconsin, and South Dakota.

". . . and the forecast calls for a ninety percent chance of rain again tomorrow."

The Midwest—the upper Mississippi River valley in particular, and those living along its tributaries—took a bath this year. The insurance company phrase "hundred-year flood plain" suddenly came to life. It's like the sign BEWARE OF DOG. You don't quite believe it till you see the snarling jaws.

". . . on that day the fountains of great deep burst forth and windows of the heavens were opened. And rain fell upon the Earth forty days and forty nights."

Especially hard hit were those who lived along the river where man had tampered with its banks. It was a humbling experience for the Corps of Engineers. Many a technical marvel disappeared like a rubber duck in a hurricane. Bridges, docks, dams, levees . . . nothing but Tinkertoys in a landfill.

"I stepped out on the front porch and the field between the house and the levee was a two-hundred-acre lake . . ."

In Coon Rapids a cowman sat on his horse last spring, his back to the driving rain. Over the hired man's shoulder he saw a white spot in the black mud. Squinting through the downpour, he recognized the spot as an eye. It was all that showed of a three-day-old calf. They dug him out, hauled him to the house, and put him in a tub of warm water. The calf was one of many of his kind that didn't make it.

". . . lower acreage, yield, and production forecast in the Crop Report . . ."

Alfalfa fields dead along the Smoky Hills River in Abilene. Farm ground so saturated for hundreds of miles that even next year's planting could be in doubt. And winter still looms ahead.

"It rained so much last night the rain gauge overflowed . . ."

The drought of '88 seems so long ago, its memory swamped by the deluge and devastation of '93. The almost unimaginable cleanup hangs over all who have been sandbagging for what seems an eternity. But as they can tell ya, rain after a dry spell is like rediscovering long-lost relatives . . . it don't take long to catch up.

"It's rainin', rainin', rainin' here this mornin', as the Mississippi flows on to the sea . . ."

Another "true story" I decorated a little. Or as they call it in my office,
Baxterizing. It's a legend, of course, in Winona, Kansas.

BALIN' WHEAT

G len said J.T. liked old pickups. But sometimes they have a mind of their own.

Early one summer morning J.T. loaded his good dog, Sam, and headed down to the wheat field. It had been cut and he planned on balin' some wheat straw as long as it still held the dew.

It was a fine western Kansas mornin'. J.T. made two passes around the wheat field before the sun burned off the moisture. He parked the 930 Case with the New Holland round baler and decided he could make it to Winona just in time for coffee shop communion. He leaped aboard his '79 Ford four-wheel-drive and cranked the engine. Unfortunately, it didn't crank back!

Starter problems, he knew. It had happened before. Something electrical that required a little short-circuiting wizardry. He raised the hood. Sam, good dog that he was, lay under the tractor waiting in the shade for his command to "Load up!"

J.T. had no manual choke, so he wedged a shotgun between the seat and the foot feed. Diggin' through his Snap-On high-tech farmer tool kit, he fished out a fence stay and a pair of pliers. He shorted the faulty electrical connection. The starter kicked over and the engine caught. It was at that moment that J.T. realized . . . the ol' '79 was in gear!

It lunged into motion. He slammed the hood and dove out of the way. Out across the wheat field it chugged, pickin' up speed. Sam came out from under the tractor tryin' to jump in the back of the truck, but it was goin' too fast.

Down through the stubble it rumbled followed by man and dog

in hot pursuit. The ol' pickup displayed an unerring sense of direction and seemed to navigate itself through the bogs, rock piles, and round bales. On several occasions when it was slowed by a mud hole or a steep rise it looked like Sam might catch up. But the pickup had lots of pasture experience and always managed to elude the pore ol' dog, who thought he was bein' left behind.

Finally it nose-dived into a washout, knocking the twelve-gauge out of position, and died of natural causes.

J.T. followed the tracks and found it facedown up against the bank. Sam was in the back where he belonged, but breathin' heavy.

J.T. eventually made it to the café around noon to tell the story. But everyone said it sure gave new meaning to the term "gunning the engine"!

This commentary inspired a good bit of mail. Raymond and Pat liked it, too, although they didn't think they were any different from anybody else. . . . They are.

THE STARR VALLEY BEAN FIELD WAR

I guess it never would have happened if Raymond hadn't sold his cows. The Starr Valley Bean Field War, I mean.

Cy talked him into planting a bean field. They both had time on their hands. The two of them would do the work. Cy put in twenty acres and Raymond furnished the machinery. The field was in a small plot of private property surrounded by the Tonto National Forest. I should point out that both men were threescore and ten . . . each.

May 10th they broke ground. That spring Arizona had above-normal moisture and the beans came on like gangbusters. Raymond left for a week, and on his return Cy was in a tizzy. Elk had invaded the bean field.

That night Raymond stood guard. He and Pat, his wife of nearly fifty years, sat in their pickup with their dogs in the back. Any approaching elk would get barked, high-beamed, and hoorahed away. Within three days the elk were comfortably grazing within ten feet of the pickup, where the bored dogs dozed through the night and the shouts were ignored.

Cy was havin' better luck durin' the day. But the beans were taking a beating. As the weeks wore on these three bean field moguls tried various methods to keep the marauding elk out of the field. They tried propane noisemakers, bonfires, highway department flashers, FM radio, and rattling feed sacks and tin plates tied in the manzanita brush. All to no avail.

They stood guard night and day for six weeks fighting a losing battle. When the beans were ready they cut 'em with Raymond's handmade rig behind the tractor. Each morning at daylight the three of them would rake the beans in a pile and pitchfork them into the pickup. Then they'd fork 'em into Raymond's rebuilt combine, an Allis-Chalmers model 60 with John Deere wheels and a plywood box.

Any piles left in the field were scattered by the elk like leaves in the fall. But the bean farmers bowed their backs and carried on. They finally finished the harvest. Back at the ranch they cleaned and "winded" them with an electric fan and wound up with eight hundred pounds of beans. Considering the expected twenty-ton harvest, I guess you could say the elk won the Starr Valley Bean Field War.

But in the eyes of Raymond, Pat, and Cy, they themselves won. They were of the generation who had walked through the Great Depression and the Second World War without a net. They had survived and left the world a better place.

We're runnin' outta these folks. They have earned our admiration and respect. I hope some of their heart and backbone is hereditary.

*This piece received quite a few letters as well, most from Milwau-
keeans, who rightly pointed out that their city, not Chicago, is the
home of bratwurst. Which I conceded.*

*However, as a travelin' man, I had occasion to eat my share in the
Chicago airport. So with apologies to Wisconsin, I can only say I
know how they feel when somebody tells me about a good Mexican
restaurant in Dubuque or Miles City.*

CHICAGO'S BRATWURST

In my travels to America's breadbasket, the great Midwest, I
have always looked forward to changing planes at O'Hare Airport. Chicago is a place where work gets done, where agribusiness is a part of the mortar and cowboys are welcome.

Chicago has a flavor all its own, and that flavor is bratwurst. I
had begun planning entire trips around this magnificent sausage
poking out the ends of a hefty workin' man's roll, beneath mounds
of sauerkraut and mustarded up. I avoided eating on the plane,
knowing the true taste of Chicago awaited me at O'Hare. It was
real food. When I took the first bite I knew where I was.

I maintain that same relish for the oyster bar in the San Fran-
cisco airport, crab cakes at Baltimore's, and breakfast at the termi-
nal in North Platte. So you can imagine my disbelief when I
stepped up to the counter in O'Hare my last visit only to be told,
"Bratwurst has been eliminated."

I backtracked to the B Concourse, desperately searching the
snack bars, only to find that, yes . . . the counterman had spoken
the truth! The bratwurst, my bratwurst, Chicago's bratwurst, had
been muscled aside by the pernicious invasion of anemic, buy-
anywhere, universal, faceless, fits-any-finger fast food. Instead of
bratwurst, in abundance was chain-store pizza, which smothered

all other smells like a dead mule in a car trunk. I was left to choose between impotent yogurt, neutral hot dogs, bottled water at $1.50 a shot, and radioactive Mexican food made with reconstituted Cheez Whiz and served on a machine-made taco shell. A complete menu available in fine malls all over the country.

Is this, I asked myself, how the disintegration of Rome began? Without bratwurst will Chicago become just another city with an airport catering to the bland masses, diving into decline, seeking the lowest common denominator for the highest dollar?

Chicago, homogenized in personality, generic in its commonness, numbing its visitors to bovine complacency, striving to mediocrity, satisfied to keep its head down and not stick out in the crowd. Is this what this proud city will become?

Will the Cubs move to Moline? Will the Board of Trade quietly sneak to St. Jo? Will the *Chicago Tribune* be bought out by *Reader's Digest*?

Chicago, thy flavor is now margarine.

Thanksgiving Day

THE NATIONAL INSECT

Thanksgiving is a time for reflection. Warm memories, overstuffed afternoons and family. Yet rising from this cornucopia of good feelings, like a rubber chicken from a shopping cart full of cut-up fryers, is that runner-up for our national bird . . . the turkey!

Despite its cinder-block-like intelligence, gurgling vocals, and dangling snood, there is nothing absurd about the turkey's being nominated as our national bird. After all, a group of entomologists tried to convince Congress to name a national insect. Their suggestion was the Monarch butterfly.

I have always assumed that the turkey was passed over for the eagle for obvious reasons: beauty, grace, majesty, strength, and inspiration. But after watching Congress consider the Monarch butterfly, I realize now it is simply a matter of which special interest group presents the most convincing case.

There was considerable rancor stirred amongst the feminist groups when they pressed their case for a national insect to represent them. They were divided between the lady bug and the queen bee. They compromised and settled on the black widow.

Organized religion sprang forth to submit their nominees. The Catholics liked the idea of a praying mantis on the fifty-cent piece. The Methodists suggested the water skipper, while the Baptists chose the lobster.

The legal profession marshaled its considerable influence behind the scorpion. Civil service employees thought the humble, diligent ant would be a good choice. Roto Rooter placed the tumblebug into consideration.

Suggestions for the national insect came pouring in from special interest groups: pork producers—the sow bug; carpenters—termite; insomniacs—bedbug; the Hunt brothers—silverfish; librarians—book lice; Nike—millipede; Republicans—the Sherman tank; Adams County bowling league—bowl weevil; uncles wanted aunts; A's wanted B's; Volkswagen wanted beetles; honky-tonkers wanted night crawlers; and the Texans thought the oil derrick would make a nice national insect!

So I can imagine if there is this much interest in a national insect, the competition must have been double tough for the national bird!

If Ducks Unlimited, the *Pelican Farm News,* the Kansas Jay-Hawkers, or Chicken of the Sea had been able to nominate candidates for the national bird, our coins might have looked a lot different!

However, if the turkey growers are still bent on installing the turkey as a symbol of something uniquely American . . . well . . . they'd have to go to Washington, D.C., anyway . . .

MOOSE ALERT

Many of the animal rights groups give awards to citizens who perform good deeds on behalf of animals. These deeds are usually along the line of rescuing mistreated horses, homeless cats, or HBC (hit by car) dogs. Rarely do any cowboys receive an award. I would like to nominate Andy for his daring moose rescue.

Andy was still trainin' on Gracie as they rode across the high mountain pasture in the Uintas that early summer day. He had named her Gracie with the same inversely convoluted reasoning with which U.S. senators refer to each other as "My distinguished colleague . . ."

They made their way along a big ditch that diverted water off the Black Fork River. Beaver dams and deadfall had made the ditch wide in spots, and the black mud would suck the sock off a frog.

Andy's herd of dogs scouted into a stand of willers and quakies where the ditch neared the river. They spooked a cow moose and her four-day-old calf. The pair ran down the ditch bank. Andy called off his dogs and followed Mama Moose and baby at an easy walk, just watchin'. Gracie snorted and pranced, unsure about the moose.

Mrs. Moose crossed the ditch above a beaver dam, but when baby followed he tangled himself in a fallen tree and got stuck. Seeing Baby Moose's dangerous predicament, Andy coaxed the nervous Gracie into the stirrup-high water. Since Andy was also checkin' the irrigation, he was wearin' his genuine Cowboy-Issue LaCross Thigh-High Waders.

Andy eased up to the calf, reached down, and pulled the stranded moosling (or is it mosling—no, then it would be meese) out by the ears. Gracie lurched, caught our daring hero off balance, and dumped him over his head.

Unbeknownst to the rescue team, Mother Moose had crossed the ditch, circled back, and snuck up on the scene of the accident. Gracie turned to free herself from the mud, looked Mrs. Moose in the eye, and fell over backwards. Square on top of Andy! He went down under the thrashing mare, fighting for his breath and pushing against Gracie.

In the next few tumultuous seconds Andy swallowed ten gallons of water, Gracie backstroked to the bank like a sand crab, and Mama Moose gathered baby and lit out for the high ground.

Andy rose periscopically from the sea spewing like a breaching porpoise. He caught sight of Gracie in full gallop, stirrups flapping, headed up the valley.

Andy slogged to the bank in his thigh-high waders full of water and collapsed.

So, whatya think? Is this story of heroism worthy of a Humane Society award? Or is it just another day in the life of one who spends his life watchin' after God's creatures? I can't say, but I'd like to have been a magpie in the cottonwood watchin'.

WHAT'S CHRISTMAS TO A COW?

I know you've prob'ly asked yourself,
*   What's Christmas to a cow?*
You've not! Well, maybe, just perchance
*   I've got you thinkin' now.*

*   When we march out on Christmas morn*
*   like nothin's goin' on,*
*   Has Yuletide struck the night before*
*   and disappeared by dawn?*

Were plastic sleeves a'hangin' up
*   around the calvin' shed?*
Did visions of molasses blocks
*   cavort inside her head?*

*   And did she lay awake at night*
*   tensed up, anticipating*
*   Or, in excitement milk her bed*
*   by accident, while waiting?*

Do cows pretend to be just cows,
*   devoid of all intrigues*
But really lead a secret life
*   like women's bowling leagues?*

*   Did we just miss the mistletoe?*
*   Did all the clues elude us?*
*   Does she believe in Santa Claus*
*   or just Santa Gertrudis?*

And if we looked would we see sign
of reindeer in the pen
Or would we just convince ourselves
the goat got out again?

And after we'd all gone to bed
would they join in a hymn
And sing that little manger song
they learned in Bethlehem?

I guess that it don't matter much
if cows believe or not.
We'll fork her out a flake of hay
and head back in a trot

To celebrate our Christmas Day
and all that we espouse
And when we say our dinner grace
we'll thank him for the cows.

For the livelihood they give us
and life we get to share
But do the cows have Christmas cheer?
Who knows, but just beware

If you see chicken tracks among
the straw and drying chips
You better check suspicious cows
for eggnog on their lips.

My old friends Tom and Leroy have figured in many of my stories. Tom was a local rancher who did daywork for Leroy, who ran one bunch of cows for the big outfit I worked for in the Northwest.

COLD FEET

Yer lookin' at a feller with no fax, no car phone, no beeper, no television, no tennis shoes, a '69 Ford pickup, an outhouse, and no flight training on a computer. But lest you lump me into that group of stodgy ol' dinosaurs that cling to the days of Faron Young, pygmy Angus, and real spare tires . . . let me assure you that I have stepped boldly into the modern world of manly footwear.

A constant recurring memory of workin' cows when I first started years ago was cold feet. Everybody wore your regular regulation cowboy boots with five-buckle overshoes. *And* everybody's feet got cold.

It was a common practice to scrape the snow and scatter straw around the squeeze chute where we were gonna be standin' all day. We'd keep a pickup runnin' with bottles of vitamin A on the dash defroster to alternate when the cold turned it thick as axle grease.

We weren't above buildin' a fire nearby to slip up to when our fingers turned to frozen hot dogs. I'd stand by the flame till the rubber on my overshoes started steamin' and my toes tingled.

But today things are different. Cowboys have benefited from NASA and the high-tech ski clothing industry. I go outside on a beautiful twenty-degree mornin' and spend all day in my insulated coveralls and moon boots. Wonderful waterproof moon boots with hard rubber soles and steel toes. Step on me, drop anvils on my feet, stand me in one place for an hour, and my toes are still toasty and safe. These boots are an invention as radical as round bales and affirmative action.

Alas, Leroy was still stuck in the five-buckle Dark Ages that late November when he and Tom completed the last circle on Yankee Bill summit lookin' for stragglers.

Four hours a'horseback in the Idaho Klondike had turned their feet to Fudgesicles. They rode up to the last gate and Leroy dismounted to let 'em through. The latch post was buttressed with big rocks. When he undid the wire gate, a twenty-pounder slid off the pile and landed on Leroy's foot.

Never one to endure pain silently, he thrashed around and fell in the snow, crying, "My toe's broke! My toe's broke!"

"Take off yer boot quick," instructed Tom, "or it'll swell!"

"But it'll freeze," whined Leroy.

"It's that or gangrene," said Tom solemnly.

"I can't ride back to camp barefooted," he complained. "It's still a mile away."

"Fill yer overshoe with snow and put it back on. It'll keep the swelling down," suggested Tom.

Leroy stood on one leg holding his manly footwear and looked up at Tom, who never cracked a smile.

When Leroy and Tom hit camp, we helped Leroy off his horse, drained the ice water out of his overshoe, and took him inside. I don't know the medical terminology to describe the condition of his foot, but we all agreed . . . it was blue.

PIG TALES

Pigs are funny. Nobody would argue about that. There are people who collect them. Pictures of them, memorabilia, statuettes, door stops, curtains, pig clocks, wallpaper, pig tails, piggy banks, pigweed, pig stickers, piglets, pig-eyed piebalds, and pygmies. In the home of a pig collector you are surrounded by pig knickknacks.

But due to my lack of experience, I have never been able to write pig poetry. When I attended veterinary school there were only three pigs west of Scott City, Kansas, and they were in the Salt Lake City Zoo. In the world of cowboy music no one has risen to claim the title "Ghost Riders in the Sty."

I have held the contention that most cowboy poetry is funny due to that close relationship between humor and tragedy. Workin' livestock is dangerous, and those of us who do it get hurt . . . a lot! So the only way to deal with the pain is to laugh about it. And you quadruple the chance of injury (and therefore humor) by adding a horse to the equation. Well, most people don't work pigs a'horseback, so you don't have as many wrecks. But where there's a will there's a way.

Ol' Mr. Schneider had a hog operation in central Missouri. He was one of the few in the country to employ dogs on the farm. Specifically, blue heelers.

One afternoon he had gathered two sows to take to the sale. Big ones, in the five-hundred-pound range. He backed his pickup to the loading chute and pulled the stock rack tailgate up.

Climbing down into the loading pen, he set the gates and began tickling and tormenting the two sows up the loading ramp. He thrashed and cursed them but they wouldn't go more than halfway. It was then he happened to look up and see his blue heeler, Bruno, sitting in the pickup bed peering down the ramp.

He shouted commands at the dog, who promptly leaped into action and started running down the ramp toward his master. The two sows began backing down and into Mr. Schneider, who was wedged in place. He went down, and one of the sows sat in his lap. The dog scaled the pileup and exited stage left.

Mr. Schneider, gasping for air and grasping for straws, did what any good cowboy would do . . . he called the dogs!

Bruno tore back around the corner, stormed up the ramp, and bit Mr. Schneider on the ham! The hogs loaded all right . . . so did Mr. Schneider, slick as you please.

Bruno is now sausage.

I have no excuse.

TOMBSTONE OF CANAAN

WANTED: A cowpoke to help gather pairs
Dogs welcome, but not if they bark
Nondrinker preferred, to help with the herd.
Signed, Noah, the U.S.S. Ark.

Now Tombstone of Canaan was broke
And, of late, had been offa the sauce.
So he rode to the yacht, was hired on the spot
And became Noah's buckaroo boss.

"Get two of each creature on Earth."
His orders were clear and precise.
To which he replied, "Does that include flies?
And roaches and woolies and mice?"

He set out like he was possessed
He roped and delivered two skunk.
Two pigs in a poke, an egg, double yoke,
Two elephants stuffed in their trunk.

Two jack eye, a double entendre.
Two fish sticks still stuck to the pan
Giraffes, neck and neck, he led to the deck
But oysters he left in the can.

He tried to get two of each specie
A male and his counterpart
But tied in the willows were twelve armadillos
'Cause he couldn't tell 'em apart.

He rode to the mountain and looked in the woods
He even went downtown a'chasin'
Did the best that he could, brought 'em back on the hood,
Two elk, two moose, and a mason.

This work had mellowed ol' Tombstone
His heart became tender and supple,
Recanting his vow, he let in a cow
And even a Methodist couple.

Then Noah took Tombstone aside,
"I'd hire you for forty more days
If I could be sure, you'd avoid the lure
Of the driftin' cowboy ways.

"I'm uneasy 'bout takin' a cowboy
Who'd pack up and leave on a whim.
Not sayin' you will, but I'd worry less, still
If I knew that you couldn't swim!"

What I describe in this story is an annual happening on farms, ranches, and small holdings around the world. Matter of fact, it is safe to say that this same procedure and these same feelings have been an occupational occurrence since man domesticated the cow eight thousand, five hundred years ago. The cow herself has changed immensely . . . on the outside. But before plastic sleeves, uterine boluses, night lights, and insulated coveralls . . . before Moses, before the Pyramids, before parliamentary procedure, E-mail, and wooden matches, animal husbandrymen were checking their heifers by moonlight. They would have roped her to a post and experienced that same nervous worry as they went in for that first exploratory palpation. And I know how they felt . . . 'cause the cow hasn't changed much . . . on the inside.

NEAT AND TIDY CALVING

This is the time of year when cow people don't get much sleep. If you boiled "raisin' cattle" down to its bare bones, the whole business revolves around gettin' a live calf on the ground.

Folks outside the wonderful world of calvin' season probably have some peculiar ideas about what happens. Maybe they think a heifer calves like chickens lays eggs. Nice and clean, no muss, no fuss. Others might picture a sterile operating room with attendants gathered around in masks and rubber gloves saying things like "Push!" and "Nurse, wipe my brow and clamp the cord!"

A neat, tidy procedure done in antiseptic surroundings, not unlike the manufacturing of venison sausage.

Neat is not the word I think of when assisting at a calving. But instead, insulated coveralls come to mind. As well as mud boots, chapped hands, rope burns, slippery chains, wet knees, sweating at ten degrees above zero, and midnight.

In fact, calving involves a whole lot more than simply inserting a coin, punching a button, and watching a can of Diet Coke be born with a thunk!

There's that businesslike confidence that guides you when you check the heifer pen before turning in. You see one that's still trying. You can't leave her in that condition all night, so you get 'er up and slog her into the trap or calvin' shed. While you're gatherin' up the O.B. chains and pullin' off your jacket, a wave of nervous worry washes over you and settles into your gut.

Anticipation builds as you reach in for your first feel around. Hope surges when you make the initial pull on the calf. If luck is on your side, an enormous sense of relief follows. If not, that sinkin' feelin' soaks in right down to your bones.

It's then that you do what your calling in life has prepared you for. It's done with all the experience, skill, compassion, and dogged determination that you possess. The buck stops on your shoulders. It's up to you and her to get the job done.

Finally, the calf comes. He plops down on the straw, wet and sleek as a porpoise. You tickle his nose; he snorts and shakes his head. You rub him down. You watch him struggle to three legs, fall, and then try again.

You pick up your stuff and back outta the pen, leavin' mama and baby alone. You stand there a minute. You hear her talk to him. She's lickin' his face.

The wind is cold on your back. Snowflakes melt on your cheek. In the presence of this miracle, you don't notice.

I wonder if dentists ever dream of working in a mouth as big as a washtub, sitting on the central incisors, bracing against a lower molar with their foot whilst chipping away like a demented diamond miner.

THE C-SECTION

The phone rang. It was four o'clock . . . the other four o'clock.
 A worried voice came on the line. "Sorry to wake ya, Doc,
But I've got a calvy heifer I think's in trouble, some.
 I can't see nothin' but the tail. I'm wonderin', could ya come?"

Next thing I know I'm in his barn and starin' at this beast.
 Ten feet tall, she was, I swear, and big as a bus, at least.
I laid a ladder 'gainst her flank. A C-section, I decide.
 After proper preparation there's a window in her side.

I poked my head inside the hole and had a look around
 A pair of parakeets flew out and fluttered to the ground,
Followed by a barkin' dog and blur of Gambel's quail.
 A hunter in fluorescent orange, hot on the covey's tail.

I climbed on in and smelled the air. No doubt, progesterone.
 I leaned against the rumen wall and heard a slide trombone!
A corps of cuds came chomping by in step with a marching band
 All tooting on a catheter. I was Alice in Kidneyland.

A school of pies came slicing by, meringues, mangos, and minces
 And dignitaries like the Queen and Michigan Pork Princess.
A set of Holstein heifers with their tassels all a'twirl.
 The sheep producers' lobbyist and Snap-On calendar girl.

On they came, the A.I. techs with pipette, fife, and drum,
   A pair of unborn senators, Fetaldee and Fetaldum.
This entire cast of characters was headed for the womb
   And ridin' drag in this parade was me behind a broom.

I passed a Winchell's Donut Shop at Pancreas and Colon
   And saw a New Age singles group reliving lives and trollin'
Then took a left on Ileum and asked the Pelvic Nerve
   Where I could find the Uterus. His Dendrite made a curve

And pointed to the Oviduct that seemed to swing and sway.
   I saw a blinking neon sign, said BABY CALF—THIS WAY.
The cotyledons bumped my head as I went slidin' down
   "There he is," I said, at last. The calf had run aground.

I hefted up a cloven hoof and started for the door.
   Then like a flash the lights came on! I slipped upon the floor.
A scream like I ain't never heard was ringin' in my head.
   I opened up my eyes and saw me standin' by the bed.

My wife was clingin' to the post all tangled in the sheets.
   The slide trombone had died away as had the parakeets.
I slowly came awake to find my dream had gone kaput.
   I looked down at her layin' there and let go of her foot!

A little satire taking us to task for loving our fragile prairies and mountains too much. And of course fiction begets truth and what I make light of in this poem is now being seriously considered to save some of our most overvisited national parks.

THE WILDERNESS WALL

If you've been losing sleep at night about the public land,
Yer not alone. We're all concerned with changes wrought by man.
The wilderness, to have and hold, is what it's all about
And we can Save the Wilderness! By keepin' people out.
By Audubon, you know I'm right. It's humans who befoul
The habitat of prairie dog, of elk and spotted owl.
A wall. We need a giant wall. To hold the riffraff back
But since they own the public lands, we'll prob'ly catch some flak,

So I propose the following: a theme park by the wall.
A simulated wilderness, man-made, au natural.
The next best thing to bein' there. We'll call it Wilderworld!
A place where you can get moosed-out, get badgered, skunked, or
squirreled!
Immerse yourself in waterfowl. Commune with ancient trees.
And though they seem so real to you, they're all facsimiles.
That's right, my friends, a theme park that's politically correct.
No tame coyotes or dancing bears to lessen the effect.

At Wilderworld *organophobes will love our guarantee,*
"No living thing was sacrificed to build this park for thee."
Imagine trees with concrete bark beneath a glassed-in dome.
Stalagmites rise from old Cheez Whiz in caves of Styrofoam.
A carbonated geyser that awaits your beck and call,
Just put a quarter in the slot and watch the water fall.
Then travel down our Nature Trail. This ride is really neat.
See hibernating bear rugs sleep and never leave your seat!

See bullfrogs made of fiberglass eye plastic dragonflies
And get the perfect snapshot 'cause they never blink their eyes.
Ceramic deer and pop-up wolves in thrilling lifelike scenes.
See automated leaping fish in bubbling brook machines.
Synthetic birds that lip-synch tunes and fly on hidden wires
While Bambi grazes AstroTurf on tiny rubber tires!
And finally, as a final treat, we've one last mem'ry planned,
Our Rangers, dressed in chipmunk suits, will eat out of your hand.

The tour just takes an hour but if you don't want to go
Just wait in the Museum Shop and buy the video
And if you're still not satisfied, when leaving you can view
The posh resort, beyond the wall, we call Camp David Two.
But you'll be sleepin' easier knowin' all the cash you blew
Will help protect the wilderness from folks like me and you.

Pickin' on another man's dog is bad etiquette in the cowboy culture. I have walked the fine line between humor and offense for years. Matter of fact, my very first collection of cowboy poetry was called The Cowboy and His Dog, or Go Git in the Pickup You S*# of a *#@*!

ADVICE COLUMN

Dear Baxter,

As a fellow veterinarian, I am hoping you can help me. My wife, Nancy, has two cow dogs that will readily obey commands to sit and stay until they get near a cow. Then they chase the critter and can't hear a word we say. It's very obvious to me that they go deaf near livestock.

So, what's your diagnosis? I've considered cow dander allergies, global warming, and ear infections, to name a few. If possible, send a shot or RX.

signed Anxious in Tie Siding, Dr. L.W.

Dear L.W.

I am pleased to inform you that your wife's two cow dogs are suffering from a malady that is common in blue heelers. It also occurs in species further down the food chain such as backyard horses, bird dogs, and teenagers.

Your suggested diagnosis associates their problems to the nearness of cattle. However, research at the NASA Cow Dog Behavioral Institute in Cabool, Missouri, indicated a relationship more closely related to the proximity of the dominant figure—i.e., the greater the distance between master and dog, the less your influence.

The technical name for the syndrome is Progressive Dumb Dog Detachment Amnesia, or PDA. There are some social scientists who believe PDA is a result of a broken home, a puppyhood trauma, or sucking hind tit. Others, with only a master's degree, prefer to think it is a biological defect like damaged chromosomes, lack of a brain, or too much Co-op dog food.

Extensive studies have been done to discover a method to change the PDA dog's behavior such as necking him to a mule, using remote-control pontoons, or letting him drag a hundred foot of log chain. Although these techniques can alter his direction, they often interfere with his mobility in the corral.

Probably the most state-of-the-art information has come from a paper presented at the prestigious PDA Symposium and BBQ in Alcova, Wyoming, by one R. Guerricabeitia, sheepherder. It is his contention that there is nothing wrong with the dog's hearing, his breeding, or his training. The PDA victim is evolving into a thinking being and has simply chosen to ignore you.

My advice: Live with it or leave him home.

This is one of those commentaries that I listen to and say, "Gosh, I wish I'd written that . . ." and then realize, I did! Outside of the coyote, border collies are the smartest animals I've been around.

This story stimulated lots of calls, reprints, and even a quote in Charles Krauthammer's column in Washington, D.C. It should always be read aloud (or at least move yer lips).

BORDER COLLIES

Just a word about one of the greatest genetic creations on the face of this earth . . . the border collie.

Faster than a speeding bullet. More powerful than a locomotive. Able to leap tall fences in a single bound.

The dog that all sheep talk about but never want to meet. The fur that legends are made of. Makes coyotes cringe, sheep trip the light fantastic, and eagles soar somewhere else.

Invested with the energy of a litter of puppies, the work ethics of a boat person, and the loyalty of Lassie, they ply their trade on sagebrush flats, grassy fields, and precipitous peaks from sea to shining sea.

"Away to me!" I command. They streak and sail, zipping like pucks on the ice. Black-and-white hummingbirds, in out, up down, come by.

Sheep. With head up, one eye cocked over their shoulder asking directions. To the gate through the race. Mighty dog moves behind the bunch like a towboat pushing barges around a bend.

And heart. Do they try? "Just let me at 'em, Dad!" Stay. "C'mon, I'm ready!" Stay. "Can't you feel me hummin'! Listen to my heart! It's purrin' like a cat! I am primed! Aim me, point me, pull the trigger!"

"Away to me!" It makes me feel like Robin Hood. He leaves my side like an arrow.

Workin' dogs is like manipulating a screwdriver with chopsticks. Like doing calligraphy with a plastic whip. Like bobbing for apples. Like threading a needle with no hands. Like playing pool on the kitchen table.

There are no straight lines in nature. Only arcs. Great sweeping curves of sight and thought and voice and dog. Always having to lead your command about a dog's length.

Sheep bunched like logs on the river. Dogs paddling in the current. Always pushing upstream. A ewe breaks loose. Then another, another. The logjam breaks. Dogs and sheep tumble about in the white water.

Calm again, they start back upstream.

Border collies. Are they truly smarter than a chimpanzee? Cuddlier than a koala? More dedicated than Batman's valet?

Can they change course in midair? Drag Nell from the tracks and locate the missing microfilm?

Yes. I believe they can. They are the best of the best, the epitome of "above and beyond the call of duty." Head dog. Top Gun. I salute you, for man has never had a better friend.

"Little Joe the Wrangler" *is a cowboy song written by Jack Thorp in 1898. My dad used to sing it to Brother Bob and me when we were kids. Every cowboy knows it.*

This commentary has been the longest (six minutes) one of mine to run on NPR, though I shortened the poem for broadcast. It is presented here in its entirety. Don Edwards, Texas balladeer, sang a verse at the end of the commentary.

The Sandhills of Nebraska is God's gift to the cowman. Except when they have a dry spell. When duty forces a man to ride the dry prairie alone . . . a good cowboy always carries a box of matches.

HE SANG "LITTLE JOE THE WRANGLER"

The dry grass crackled underfoot, was dang near stirrup-high.
The horse and rider left a wake as they went riding by.
Their shadow swam beneath the horse, no elbows stickin' out.
The hoppers thick as dirt road dust, the prairie sick with drought.

No cattle in this section piece. They stayed down by the creek.
The rider only rode to see how bad it was this week.
Due east across the grassy sea he rode with squinting eyes.
No cloud to break the baking heat, but then to his surprise

The slightest shadow fell across the ground on either side.
He stirred from somnolescent thought, from soporific ride.
His senses came alert and he sat straighter in the seat.
The blue sky had a pinkish tinge . . . and then he felt the heat.

He swung his horse back to the west and saw the wall of flame.
The god of fire was hot to trot and back to stake its claim.
It felt like his whole head caved in as blood drained from his
brains.
The fist of fear that gripped his heart squeezed dread into his
veins.

They wheeled as one and in two jumps were flying 'cross the plain.
They ran flat out for near a mile but hardly did they gain
For now the fire was like a mob that fed upon its own,
Self-conflagrating cannibals cremating flesh and bone.

The smoke was in his horse's nose, the fear was in his eyes.
The froth blew off his heaving flanks and soon was vaporized.
A hole, a hump, a hidden clump, whatever . . . jammed the gear.
The horse went down like he'd been shot! The rider landed
clear.

The flames hung down like curtains there behind the fallen horse.
The beast was struggling to his feet, the wind was gaining force.
The rider dug a wooden match from out his sweaty shirt
And struck it on his zippered fly, then reached down to the dirt

And lit a clump of tinder grass without a second thought.
In moments with the steady breeze the helpless prairie caught.
The horse in panic tried to run but couldn't bear his weight.
His right hind packed up under him. The rider didn't wait.

He peeled his shirt off with a tug and quickly tied a blind
Around the faunching horse's head to try and calm his mind.
The spot he'd lit was fanning out but in its wake lay bare
A blackened smoking patch of ground that beckoned to the pair.

With coaxing-pulling-pounding will he danced the horse around
  Until they stumbled through the ring and stood on burnt-off
    ground.
He jerked his rope down from the horn and talking all the time
  He sidelined up the good hind foot to drop him on the dime.

Then pulled him down and dallied up and somehow with the rest
  Reached down and looped the left front foot and pulled it to his
    chest.
He looked up at the raging fire that towered overhead.
  The wind that beat hard on his face now pressed his back instead.

The fire was sucking oxygen to feed its hungry forge.
  The backdraft fueled the dragon's flame that bore down on
    St. George.
With nylon rope and reins in hand the rider cuddled near.
  He lay beside the stricken horse and sang into its ear,

. . . He's Little Joe the wrangler, boys . . . *the fire became a roar.*
  It rose up like a cobra's hood . . . he'll wrangle never more . . .
The sky turned black . . . An OK spur from one foot lightly
    hung . . .
  The devil's furnace set on high but still the cowboy sung

. . . The boss he cut him out a mount . . . *like bugs caught in a
      yawn*
  They lay in the volcano's throat . . . and kindly put him on . . .
Surrounded by a ring of fire they clung to their domain,
  Two captives on a railroad track beneath a passing train

. . . He's ridin' ol' Blue Rocket with a slicker o'er his head . . .
  The peak of the inferno was enough to wake the dead.
The rider tugged the shirt on down to wrap the horse's nose.
  His voice raw, he whisper-sang and kept his own eyes closed

... But one of us was missin', boys ... *By now he'd worn a groove.*
Together there, just mouth to ear, the pony never moved
... Next mornin' just at daybreak ... *Then the wind began to turn.*
The rider felt a different breeze, his cheeks began to burn

... Beneath him mashed into a pulp ... *Still trapped in his own hell*
The rider croaked his scraping dirge ... His spur had wrung the knell ...
How long he held the horse's head no one could really know.
And on he sang ... Our little Texas stray poor Wrangler Joe ...

———————

The pilot finally spotted them and radioed the ground.
The boys who reached him in the truck weren't sure what they had found.
The horse was layin' on his side, his head a'pointin' north.
The rider hunkered over him just rockin' back and forth.

The T-shirt burnt clean off his back, his bare head fairly scorched.
The horse's hair was singed like wool, his mane and tail torched.
The pair smelled like a brandin' fire but what disturbed the boys
Was comin' from the rider's lips, a scratchy humming noise.

A raspy ragged lullaby that carried on the air
And slithered up their prickled necks and held them frozen there.
Before them grinned the face of death, the Earth, its skin unpeeled.
The world consumed by fire this time, Apocalypse revealed.

184

But beating in this ruined place two hearts somehow prevailed
   And hung in balance by a thread, a sigh could tip the scales.
Then Jim eased up, like you would do a spooky colt, perhaps,
   And touched him with an outstretched hand . . . the rider just
      collapsed.

This tale was told in countless camps where killin' time's the rule.
   Some say the rider was insane and babblin' like a fool.
But Jim, who reached the rider first was haunted his life long
   With "Little Joe the Wrangler" . . . But, who knows . . . it's just
      a song.

This piece presents the spirit and independence a lot of us from the West are proud of. It also says something about why small western towns become self-sufficient . . . the geography and the fact that less than 4 percent of the population of the United States lives in the Mountain Time Zone.

And, though I did get one letter complaining about how I was pickin' on Mrs. Clinton, it would have been nice to have her there.

THE OUTBACK

P arts of Montana are as close to the Outback as "Yanks" will ever get.

They had given me directions in the Hell Creek Bar. Next mornin' I was tryin' to decipher my scribbling from the back of a napkin. I turned off the paved road at Cohagen. My new friends had specifically told me to go six miles (one said seven), then turn south. "Can't miss it," they assured me, "straight shot to Forsyth."

At six miles on the odometer there it was, just like they said. The only problem was, a hundred yards south of the turn the road forked . . . Big Time! Both forks were well traveled, pointed south, and disappeared over the horizon.

I backed up to the six-mile corner to regroup and spied a contrail of dust comin' my way. I flagged the driver down. It was the Garfield County agent. He directed me to bear right at the fork. We drove off in opposite directions. I didn't pass another car for fifty-three miles.

It's been a long time since I've done that. In the middle of a workin' day, I drove fifty miles and never passed another car.

The layered horizons were festooned with buttes and rock formations that looked like giant tepees. The vast expanse was virtually treeless. You could spot the occasional creek by the cottonwoods that followed its meandering course.

The clover was in bloom. I surfed through big lakes of yellow blossoms. Baby antelope twins bounced through the sagebrush like jackrabbits trailing their sleek moms.

Now and then, I'd pass a bunch of cows. I slowed for a pair of skittery gray geldings. Disinterested sheep ignored my intrusion. Hawks, Canadian geese, and killdeer circled and scattered in my path.

Jordan, Montana, was celebrating the grand opening of the Garfield County (pop. 1,500) Health Center. The festivities had been a typical community effort. Hundreds of people showed up. After all, it was their health center.

Even though the county has no medical doctor, the center maintains a medical staff including nurses and a physician's assistant. They are in contact by phone with doctors.

It is a ranching community of people who know their ancestors and each other's kids. They can spot a pilgrim, a tourist, or a government man with ease, mostly because they know everybody else who lives there. And even in a state that prides itself on its hardiness and independence, they consider themselves the keepers of the flame. Saddle bronc riders come from Jordan. Bareback riding is for pansies.

Sometimes it is easy to be overwhelmed by the continuing barrage of news stories about the homeless and helpless, the irresponsible and ignorant, the lazy and parasitizing. I get frustrated by well-meaning, condescending social engineers prescribing Band-Aids for compound fractures of the human condition. If people are told often enough that they can't take care of themselves, they give up.

But in Jordan, at the grand opening of their health center, my faith was renewed. It occurred to me as I watched these self-reliant citizens take care of their own, it's too bad Hillary couldn't be here.

Intermittent Stream Ranch lays between Ted's Corner and the Wyoming line in northern Colorado. When I saw the sign, I couldn't believe it either!

TRUTH IN LABELING

We were headed up a back road the other day and passed a sign that gave us pause. It read INTERMITTENT STREAM RANCH.

Butch and I discussed whether possibly these folks were the victims of a new truth-in-labeling law hatched by some busybody bureaucracy. Could Intermittent Stream Ranch originally have been Dry Creek Ranch? Or even Stuttering Brook Farms? We began to look for other names that might fall prey to these picky-picky pontificrats.

The Mile High City. Colorful, descriptive, but certainly not completely truthful. Truth-in-labeling might require Denver to rename itself the Somewhere-in-the-Neighborhood-of-a-Mile-High City.

How 'bout the Mississippi River? Wouldn't it be more accurate were it called the Ten-State Contiguous Cooperative Drainage System (and Bait Shop)?

Advertising a Manure Spreader might be less confusing if the advertiser distinguished between a person and piece of machinery. Truth-in-labeling would dictate they be more specific—i.e., a Consulting Economist versus a Bovine Night Soil Disseminator.

Chicken pox. Not only inaccurate but a slam to the poultry industry as well as the Pox family in Green Forest, Arkansas. Kid spots is what they should be.

Freeway. At over a million dollars a mile it should be called the Santa Monica Expenseway.

Does "religious right" mean they are correct all the time and "the liberal left" mean he's gone for good?

Are the names Garden City, New York City, and Des Moines really descriptive of the towns? Would a stranger pullin' off Kansas Highway 50 through the wheat and feedlots suddenly exclaim, "This town is a garden spot! It surely must be Garden City!"

In truth, New York City is Old York, and I've never seen a moin in Des Moines. Why not call it Des Corns or Des Pigs?

Truth-in-labeling. Once they get started it will never end. We'll have to change the name of the hotdog, cowboy, gay caballero, and pork princess. Shoot, I might even have to change my name to Frontster Caucasian, Livestock Husbandry Person Versifier.

Herding sheep in the last several decades in the West has always been the province of Basque people. They came from Spain on work permits of three to seven years. Lately, South American immigrant herders, mostly from Peru, have begun to move into the job of herding the large bands of sheep. It seems half of all the herders I have known are named Juan.

IT'S THE LAW

There is a state law on the books in Colorado that makes it illegal for a sheepherder to abandon his sheep without notice.

A good law, really, since herders are often left alone on isolated ranges with their entrusted band. The owner or boss usually checks on him once a week or so and brings him supplies. So, it would certainly create serious consequences were the sheep to be deserted and untended for any length of time.

But, to the uninformed—nonsheep people, that is—this law might seem a little unclear.

It could be interpreted to mean that the herder must notify his sheep before leaving them, to prevent emotional trauma, possibly, social breakdown, or obscure ovine behavioral disorders.

To comply with the law, he might line them up and give a sort of "going away" speech:

"My fellow ewes, lambs, and bucks. I have called you together to make an announcement. At approximately noon today, I intend to abandon you.

"It has not been an easy decision. I lay in my camp pondering the effect it would have on the herd. I agonized over leaving something we've both worked so hard to establish. The caring and sincere bond we've formed that has made my job such a pleasure. The chuckles we've had and the times we've cried.

"I've asked a lot of you. At lambing, marking, and shearing, not to mention the time you all got footrot. Tough times. But you all gave it your best effort and survived. And, I think, y'all are better sheep for the experience.

"But people, just like sheep, grow and change. My needs are different, my horizons have expanded. I hope to enroll in a welding course at Community College and follow my star.

"I'm leaving you in good hands—or hooves, as it were. Paulita, I expect you to take over. You've been a strong example to the other ewes. Always first to water, first to new grass, and always willing to listen to the baa's and bleatings of others.

"Leadership is not an easy mantle to wear. And followers, you too, must blindly trust your leader and follow her like . . . well, like sheep.

"You must work as a cohesive unit, sticking to the instinctive survival traits of prey, always remembering, just like in any bureaucracy, that the group is more important than the individual. It is your strength and will prevent you from becoming another fractionated, dysfunctional herd.

"In conclusion, it was just my job. To protect you from predators: coyotes, the BLM, deer hunters, and the like. But your gratitude is humbling. That gratitude is what I will carry with me from this day forward. Words cannot express my thanks for your overwhelming display of affection. After all, how many of us can claim to have six hundred ram lambs named Juan in their honor?"

(Thanksgiving Day)

THE FIRST COWBOY THANKSGIVING

In November 1621, a Thursday, I believe, the pilgrims were fixin' to set down to a meager meal of fish sticks and boiled beets. When out of the woods marched a jovial band of Indians packin' a bushel of roastin' ears and two wild turkeys. Thursday, Thanksgiving, as we know it today, was born.

But what if those generous Indians had chosen to take their bounty to the wild game feed at the VFW, instead? And in their place the pilgrims were met by a crew of cowboys on their day off?

These prerevolutionary buckaroos would have passed around their own Wild Turkey. Soon as everybody was tuned up and visitin' like used-car salesmen, preparations would have been made for chuck. They'd have barbecued a couple Spanish goats, some buzzard jerky, a side of javelina, and a bucket of quail. Not to mention a jackrabbit they'd run over on the way into camp.

As a special treat they'd have thrown a few Rocky Mountain oysters on the hot rock for hors d'oeuvres. I can just see the young, single, upwardly mobile Pilgrim girls gigglin' and gnawin' on a piece of javelina haunch.

Toasts would have been made to all the greats: Christopher Columbus, John Smith, John Alden, Casey Tibbs, James Fenimore Cooper, John Elway, Bob Wills, Sir Walter Raleigh, Jerry Palen, Pocahontas, and Francis Scott Key. No cowboy gatherin' would be complete without a fiddle. The cowboys might have taught 'em the two-step and the cotton-eyed Joe. The Pilgrims would reciprocate with the minuet and Turkey in the Straw.

No doubt, Paul "Rawhide" Revere would have snuck Priscilla over to Sooner Rock (two hundred yards up the beach from

Plymouth Rock, discovered by two Okies who stowed away on the Mayflower and jumped ship early, claiming the continent for Pawhuska) for a little spoonin.'

By dawn they'd all be sayin' good-bye and promising to meet again next year.

If that scenario had occurred, Thanksgiving would be different today. It would be more like a combination of New Year's Eve and Custer's last stand. Every November we'd be sittin' down to a table bristlin' with brisket and beans. The centerpiece would be the traditional cow skull, and afterwards everybody would have a piece of armadillo mince pie.

However, the turkey would not have been lost completely. It would have become the symbol of another national celebration that stops the country in its tracks and gives us pause to think . . . Election Day!

*I've always been disappointed that no one from KMUW in Wichita
ever called.*

THE REINDEER FLU

You remember that Christmas a few years ago
  When you waited all night for ol' Santy to show?
Well, I heard the reason and it just might be true
  The whole bunch came down with the dang reindeer flu.
The cowboy elves had been busy all day
  A'doctorin' Donner and scatterin' hay.
Dancer and Prancer were febrile and snotty
  Comet and Cupid went constantly potty.
Hallucinatory dementia was rampant
  Why, Blitzen imagined that he was Jed Clampett.
Dasher got schizo and thought he was Trigger
  While Vixen's obsessions got bigger and bigger.
By noon Santy knew they should find substitutes
  So the cowboy elves went out searching recruits.
They scoured the Arctic for suitable prey
  And brought them together to hook to the sleigh.
When Santy climbed up it was like a bad dream
  He stared down the lines at the substitute team.
A bull moose as old as the planks on the ark
  With a head as big as a hammerhead shark
Stood hitched by a cow, Mrs. Santy's, of course,
  Then next in the tugs was a Clydesdale horse.
He was paired with an elk whose antlers were crossed
  An ostrich, a walrus, an old albatross
Were harnessed in line but the last volunteer
  Was a blue heeler dog with only one ear.

The cowboy elves gave a push to the sled
  As Santy rared back, cracked his whip, then he said,
"On Cleo, on Leo, on Lefty and Jake,
  On Morphus, Redondo, on Lupe and Snake . . ."
Smoke from the runners cut tracks in the snow
  The team headed south, but, where else could they go?
They started back east 'cause it got dark there first
  And their luck, which was bad, got progressively worse.
By the time they hit Kansas the tugs had gone slack
  And all but the dog was now ridin' in back.
Santy was desperate. What on earth could he do?
  Then the lights of an airport hove into his view.
Did they make it? You betcha, but here hangs the tale
  Of how, on that Christmas, they stayed on the trail.
A man in Alaska said right after dawn
  A low-flying object passed over his lawn.
He ran to the window and threw up the sash
  and heard someone shouting, "Fer Pete's sake, don't crash!
On Budget, on Thrifty, look out Alamo
  I didn't take out the insurance, you know.
And you, Number Two, try harder, yer Avis.
  On Dollar, on Hertz, Rent-a-Wreck, you can save us
An extra day's charge if we make it by nine
  Though the drop-off will cost us a bundle this time.
Merry Christmas," *yelled Santy, but he was all smiles*
  'Cause at least he'd signed up for unlimited miles.
So that's how it happened as best I recall
  When it looked like that Christmas might not come at all.
And the truth of the matter, we all owe a cheer
  To the Wichita office of Rent-a-Reindeer.

You can't make up this kind of stuff. Inspiration abounds in the cowboy world.

COWBOY MENTALITY

I ran into Randy in the airport. He was draggin' his right hind leg like an escaped convict tryin' to cover his tracks. I could see it had taken him a while to pull his pant leg on over the swollen knee. He side-slid to a stop to visit for a minute.

"So," I asked stupidly, "hurt yourself?"

Randy is a rodeo announcer. A good one, I might add. I've seen him work. But this injury could certainly not be work-related, I thought to myself. Rodeo announcers are a little higher up the food chain than those of us who actually get within striking distance of large herbivores. They sit in their ivory towers above the dust and flailing hooves, inciting the fans and titillating the timers. Occasionally stooping to act as straight man to the barrel man's jokes, but above it all, maintaining their dignity. Ringmaster of all they survey.

He gave me a raised eyebrow, realized that I was not smart enough to have asked the question facetiously, and explained. In an effort to "keep up with the competition" he had taken to announcing rodeos a'horseback.

"Say no more," I thought. Riding a strange horse furnished by the stock contractor into the center of the arena surrounded by thousands of foot-stompin', whistlin', avid rodeo fans, reins in one hand, microphone in the other, with flags flyin', banners flappin', and music blarin' . . . the outcome is almost predictable.

His story included all of that and concluded with a wild bucking exit where he bailed out with the grace of a sandbag fallin' off the back of a runaway stagecoach.

What makes people do things like that says something about the cowboy mentality. This mentality is best characterized by that old joke where the guy holds his hand in front of his face and bets his friend that he can't "hit my hand before I move it."

I've been wearing a neck brace for several weeks. Not in public, of course. Maybe I wouldn't be so reluctant to wear it if I didn't have to respond to the question . . . "So, did you hurt your neck?"

What do I tell them? No. It's just decorative. A cosmetic article of clothing designed to offset my bad posture and enhance my fine facial features. Or maybe . . . my wife gave it to me on our tenth anniversary . . . or, I wrenched it saving a school bus load of children from a burning building.

If I was forced to explain, I would have to say I was riding down the trail with an amigo whose horse was jiggin' and tossin' his head. So I told this amigo that he didn't have to put up with that kind of unsavory equine behavior. When he throws his head, I said, conk him between the ears. "Whattya mean?" asked my amigo. So I demonstrated by leaning out of the saddle and whacking his horse on the poll with a thirty-two-ounce mug I'd got at the Git and Go. The mug broke, his horse stampeded, and when I straightened up, I couldn't move my neck.

See what I mean? Randy's story isn't that preposterous after all. Just part of the cowboy way. Here, bet you can't hit my hand before I move it.

Update: Annual registration for the trailer is now only eleven dollars.

THE VALDEZ

Lately there has been dissension at the rancho. I have overheard murmurings in the barnyard, in particular regarding my stock trailer. The grumbling animals enlisted my teenage daughter, Jennifer, to present their complaints.

In my defense let me describe my trailer. I felt like it was a real bargain when I bought it. Let's see, in 1986. It's a sixteen-foot Hale '71 model with a bumper hitch. Upon purchasing it from a reputable Hereford breeder who guaranteed it would haul up to eight full-grown cows, I made a few minor repairs.

Three of the wheel bearings needed replacing but the left front still spun good. We welded a jack on the tongue, built a new wooden panel for the end gate, put plywood over the rotting floor, and bought inner tubes for the two new recaps that didn't have any tread left.

I'm still working on the wiring and have got a good coat of primer on the front panel that covers about six square feet in the shape of Utah. The greenish primer almost matches the original scour yellow.

Recently I put down a rubber mat on the slick plywood after a horse came loose in transit and slid from front to back goin' up a steep grade. Every improvement an investment, I always say.

Jennifer's list of complaints seem trifling. The horses, she claims, are embarrassed to be seen unloading. She suggested I repaint it. Trying to get along, I pulled it down to the sandblasting guy for an estimate. He recommended against it. Apparently he was afraid it would cause structural damage. To remove that much rust would weaken the steel.

Admittedly there has been some erosion where the sheet metal sides attach to the frame. This complaint was brought up by the cows. They worried about sliding a foot through the four-inch gap that circles the trailer. I have always looked on that gap as good drainage to prevent manure buildup. I take it the boys at the sale barn agree since they've named my trailer the Valdez.

The dogs only asked that they be allowed to stay in the cab of the pickup instead of shut up in the trailer when I go into the sale. That way if they see any other dogs they can duck below the dash. I thought leavin' them in the trailer would keep other dogs from peein' on the tires. But they said no self-respecting dog would even consider it.

Perhaps my daughter has her own motives. I've noticed she won't even tie her horse to the trailer at a ropin' or horse show. I offered to paint her name on the side. Give her some pride of ownership. She said no thanks. I've always admired her modesty.

Bein' a good ranch boss, I'm considering their grievances, but I've good reason to avoid any hasty decisions. The Valdez is perfectly suited to my pickup. It's a '69 Ford with good tires and a fully functional left side mirror. Besides, the annual registration for the trailer is only thirteen dollars.

This is one of those poems that occasionally escape from my pen. The letters I received regarding this commentary, though not a landslide, were certainly passionate. It must strike a nerve with some folks.

THE MOUNTAIN

Nobody rides the Mountaintop when Winter's locked her jaws.
  The Mountain bears the brunt alone, his shoulder to the claws.

  She carves great gashes down his flank like butchers flensing
      sheep
      And howl, you cannot know the word. She never lets him sleep.

And on his peak she wreaks her wrath. He reaches Heaven-bound
  But she has placed a crown of ice and turned Hell upside down.

  My parka hood is fringed with frost. It's hard to get my wind.
    I stand hard on the timberline feeling freshly skinned.

The sweat is drippin' down my neck. It's twenty-two below.
  I came to tell the Mountaintop, "Just three more months to go."

  "You're not alone," *I shout to him.* "There's others just like you
      Who make their stand upon the Earth and see the battle
      through

The daily grind to just get by against all Earthly odds
    And keep the faith though they might feel forsaken by the
      gods."

  My words are snatched up by the wind and shatter in the air.
    The Winter scatters spoken broken pieces everywhere.

I strain to see the highest ridge that climbs the steep terrain
  That's whipped until its frothy edge is like a horse's mane

  Then disappears into the storm, the maelstrom, the shriek,
    That smothers and obliterates the nearly hidden peak.

The Winter bellows out her rage. She's comin' down the face.
  I turn downhill and cower in the timber's tall embrace.

  Her blizzard fingers flow around the trees and follow me.
    I stop and squint back toward the top but white-out's all I see.

I meant to bring some small relief. I wanted just to say
  No man or mountain stands alone, we're all the Maker's clay.

  "But I can only cringe and squeak," *I whisper up the slope*
    But then the Mountain answered back, "Go, friend. You left
    me hope."

It is with a sigh of relief I can relate that my veterinary career rarely included hogs or chickens. Nothing personal, just that they were rare in a ranch and feedlot practice in the West. I like pigs best as pork, and I have nothing against poultry—I eat every egg I can. It's one less chicken I have to contend with.

OF PIGS AND POULTRY

W hen hog producers called themselves "the other white meat," I don't think they figgered that someday it would be the same price.

But these unrelated species have much in common. They are easily distinguished from the munching, nibbling, cud-chewing, dull-witted herbivores that also appear in the photo album of the family farm.

While cows and sheep require expanses of pasture or mountains of roughage to fuel their bubbling, gurgling rumens, pigs and poultry are able to exist on high-energy compact concentrates. It is misleading to label them simple-stomached animals. It is their evolutionary pot of gold to digest high-protein diets that has placed them, gustatorily speaking, higher up the food chain. Omnivores, they are . . . like people.

This trait has allowed them to be concentrated in confinement barns. To be fed strictly controlled rations and managed intensely. To that end they have been genetically selected so that they look, grow, and perform like peas in a pod. The finished product is a consistent package of bacon or bag of chicken wings, the ultimate consumer desire.

It is interesting that on the graph of animal intelligence they diverge. A pig is to a chicken as a cowboy is to a sheep, like a border collie is to a turkey or a cow is to a rock. But what good has this intellect done for either species? They still spell ham and eggs.

In the arena of Old West romance, neither pigs nor poultry has fared well. The cow has walked off with all the good acting roles. There are no songs dramatizing a thundering stampede of trampling Durocs with Little Joe the Swineherd riding ol' Blue Rocket to turn the shoat in the lead. Granted, the Little Red Hen has given chickens their moment in the sun, but usually they are stereotyped as frenzied Chicken Littles.

And yet here they sit in the modern world as examples of animal science at its best. And one day soon they will achieve that final accolade of high-tech recognition. To have an automobile named in their honor like the Mustang, the Ram, or the Limousine. But until that time they must content themselves to be represented by home appliances or garden tools like the deep-fat fryer or the wheelbarrow.

This piece elicited several times the comment, "I nearly drove off the road." It is better presented orally. So, at least read it out loud and think of yourself as selling Veg-o-matics!

COW XTRACTOR

Ladies and Gentlemen! How many times have you been leading your cow down the street and suddenly looked back to find her with a foot stuck in the storm drain?

Or taken her to a nice neighborhood tavern only to have her catch a hoof behind the foot rail at the bar and create a scene? You need COW XTRACTOR!

Yes, the genuine, patented, must-have, bovine-tested, ruminant-approved, guaranteed-not-to-curdle-the-milk, fits-any-finger COW XTRACTOR.

Sure, you're saying, COW XTRACTOR will work on small cows like the Jersey-Southdown cross, but what if you're the owner of a Four-Wheel-Drive Chianina-Caterpillar composite with a head like the bucket on a front-end loader and feet the size of Humvee rims?

COW XTRACTOR has a solid-gold guarantee. Just return the unused portion with an eight-by-ten glossy of your un-xtracted cow and an affidavit signed by a certified COW XTRACTOR technician in your area and we will rush Lars Narsveld, our international COW XTRACTOR XPERT, to your home, farm, or place of business with his backhoe and Handyman jack to consult with you on how to properly xecute the COW XTRACTOR.

We are awash in testimonials from satisfied customers.

Says Joe in Tulare: "My cow was stuck in a rut. Get up, eat, give milk, sleep, get up, eat, give milk, sleep . . . over and over. She became depressed. COW XTRACTOR changed all that. Now she's taking classes at Community College in Interspecies Relations."

And from Joe in Bartlesville: "I had a cow that got stuck in the crotch of a pecan tree twenty foot off the ground. Even the paramedics from Nowata couldn't entice her down. COW XTRACTOR saved the day!"

Yessir! COW XTRACTOR can xtract your cows out of: a womb, the nose of a tractor trailer, a mesquite thicket, a well casing, a deer blind, a Chevy Suburban, a snowbank, a pool hall, a bear trap, a Powder River panel, a portable dipping vat, a yard sale, a ten-cow pileup, the neighbor's pasture, the neighbor's meat freezer, hog wire, a flatbed, the Homecoming float, sorting alley, loading chute, poetry gathering, cabinet meeting, or bad relationship.

No farm or ranch should be without COW XTRACTOR.

As Joe from Okeechobee says:

> *"I've tried it all from wrecking ball*
> *to dynamite and tractor.*
> *But when she's stuck I've had good luck*
> *by using COW XTRACTOR."*

So, there you have it in a nutshell. Order yours today so next time you won't be caught saying, "Now's when we need COW XTRACTOR."

There are several dead poets whose work I admire, like Banjo Paterson, Henry Lawson, and Rudyard Kipling. One of my favorites is Robert Service, who wrote of the Frozen North during the Gold Rush. I was influenced by his style when I wrote this poem.

THE HUNTER'S SON

This is the poem of the hunter's son as he tracks the woods alone
  And the beaver's revenge when he seeks to avenge the
    hunter's gauntlet thrown
      By choosing to pair with a grizzly bear, big, nasty and fully
        grown.

He was raised in the woods and meadow where ice and forest collide
  In the Peace River reach where fathers still teach their sons how
    to hunt and provide.
Young Scott was in search of the beaver. The country was thick with
    'em then.
  Traps were his love but he wasn't above a rifle shot now and
    again.

He snuck through the woods like a shadow and stopped just short of
    a spring.
There on the bank like a person of rank sat Oscar, the Beaver King.
  He was big as a Yellowknife huskie and hummin' a
    Rachmaninov.
Scott froze in his tracks, Oscar never looked back till he heard the
    safety click off.

Then he rolled like a log to the water. The bullet sang just by his ear
    Though caught unaware he escaped by a hair and Scott saw the
        King disappear.
Scott cursed his bad luck 'cause ol' Oscar had beaten him just like
    before
    So he turned on the trail, like a dog tuckin' tail, and headed back
    home sad and sore.

    But his path was impeded in progress by a bear with a griz
        pedigree.
He was hungry and large, so when he made a charge Scott climbed
    up a poplar tree.
    He clum till the tree started bendin', twenty feet up off the ground.
He sat in a crotch while the bear carved a notch each time that he
    circled around.

He climbed within inches of Scotty and scared the beejee outta him,
    He snorted and growled and about disemboweled the poplar tree,
    root to limb.
But he finally backed off, reconsidered, like only a grizzly bear could,
    He shook a big paw and bid au revoir, then disappeared into the
    wood.

    Though shaken, Scott felt he had triumphed, there from his perch
    in the bleachers.
The vast human brain will always remain the master of God's lesser
    creatures.
    But the sight he beheld left him chastened, outwitted by
    overachievers.
The bear reappeared, new help commandeered, with Oscar, the
    King of the Beavers.

My producer in 1995, Tom Goldman, asked me to review a cassette put out by CMH Records. It was called Doggone Country. *I had fun doin' it, but it's hard for me to be too critical. Having had my writing be the object of critics' wrath, I know it can hurt people's feelings.*

DOGGONE COUNTRY

First let's examine the premise of the album . . . *country songs about dogs.* An interesting choice considering the other possibilities: *Easy-listening songs about condo leasing, blues songs about bodies of water, heavy metal songs about alternative uses for kitchen appliances, or polkas played by bands whose names end with the letter K.*

I expect the producers had it narrowed down to *country songs about dogs, drunks, or trains* and chose to go with dogs because dog owners tend to be a bigger segment of the record-buying public than drunks or frequent flyers of Amtrak.

And it is a proven market—dog owners, that is. One that has been plundered shamelessly by artists, book writers, rawhide salesmen, and knickknack vendors since Buffalo Bill invented the chew toy. Christmas shopping in a pet store always seems a little twisted to me.

This marketing approach assumes that if you have a dog you'll love this album. Well . . . there are different kinds of dogs. And to further define its appeal let me mention a few of the recording artists featured: Doc Walsh and the Carolina Tar Heels, Gid Tanner and the Skillet Lickers, and Al Hopkins and the Buckle Busters. Okay, that should give you a clue.

There is an abundance of bluegrass hound dog huntin' songs. My favorite of which is on this album. Grandpa Jones singin' "Ol' Rattler's Treed Again" [here we played a cut from "Ol' Rattler"].

For those of us who grew up playing country music it was almost obligatory that you learn "Ol' Shep." You could always sing it and make somebody cry. This album contains "Ol' Shep" plus a couple more tearjerkers—"I Found My Best Friend in the Dog Pound," sung by Burl Ives, and "Dad Gave My Dog Away," written and sung by T. Texas Tyler—that could be a model for every self-important preachy folk song or movie that blatantly browbeats our social conscience. Eat your heart out, Oliver Stone [here we played a cut from "Dad Gave My Dog Away"].

Ah, you gotta love a song where the dog's name is Bruce.

Actually, I enjoyed the album. I like bluegrass and country, and I like dogs. I played the album for Boller, Bailey, and Hattie, my cow dogs. They particularly liked the howling part. And there is plenty of howling on it.

But lest I leave you with the impression this is just a pleasant listen-to-once-and-give-away kinda tape, there is one cut that raised the hair on my back and made me sniff the air. I guess it was such a surprise amongst its littermates, I was taken aback. It was worth the whole album. Take a listen to the Eddie Adcock band playin' "Dog" [here we played cut from "Dog"].

If that don't make you wanna start markin' yer territory, I don't know what will.

Man, this one did attract attention. I'm not sure what made it stick in the listener's ear, but people are still asking for reprints. It is, of course, a true story. Without identifying him, Don is a middle-aged rancher in Alberta who had been forced back into the "dating scene" after many years. But a lot of us have been there and can relate.

THE ROMANTIC COWBOY

There's nothing like an evening of calving to promote the romantic image of the cowboy. Right, ladies?

Don invited a nice woman out to his ranch one evening for candlelight, wine, and canned bean dip. This dinner date coincided with calving season. After an hour of civilized conversation about French painting, the European Common Market, and the condition of the rodeo arena in Ponoka, Don invited his date to go with him to check the cows.

She didn't exactly squeal with delight, but he explained how scientific livestock raising had become. "Almost like visiting a human hospital maternity ward," he said authoritatively.

They drove his Bronco out into the calving pasture and immediately spotted a braymer-cross cow tryin' to calve. "We'll watch her for a few minutes to see if everything comes out okay," suggested Don, sliding an arm around his date's shoulders.

They sat in the warm cab, moonlight mixing with Don's elaborate discourse of bovine parturition. After half an hour he decided to assist the cow. Partly for the cow and partly to show off.

The calf appeared to be hiplocked.

His date was prepared to see Marcus Welby save the day. Don drove up to the head end of the cow and left the headlights shining in her eyes. Sneaking out, he slipped around behind her. He slid the nylon obstetrical straps over the calf's protruding front feet. At first tug the cow arose like a bee-stung buffalo.

She whirled to mash Don. He was jerked off his feet but clung to the straps as the cow chased him like a dog chasin' its tail. He was alternately upright, flat out, levitating, scooting, skiing, sliding, screaming, and squirreling as the three of them circled like a shaky ceiling fan.

His only hope of survival was to hang on and stay behind the helicoptering cow. She managed to land enough blows to win the round and tromp his fallen hat to a pulp.

On one mighty jerk, the calf popped out. Don executed a complete cartwheel and landed on his back. The cow rolled him once and headed off into the darkness.

His date, who had watched Don's calving technique from the cab, was not impressed. "Less than professional," she had commented as he climbed into the cab after giving the departed cow a four-alarm cussing.

Don tried to regain his composure and recapture the mood by explaining that he had been in control the whole time. However, it was not very convincing what with the big glob of manure plastered on the side of his neck and the piece of placenta dangling from his ear.

Another true story. I speak in many small communities. I have noticed that for any little town to survive, they have to have a handful of people willing to work. It's the same 10 percent who do everything. They put on the community theater, the county fair; they run for county commissioner, serve as deacon in the church; they're on the school board, president of the Rotary, in the livestock association, on the fund-drive committee, and anyplace they're needed . . . usually without pay.

It doesn't always go smoothly.

A COWBOY PARADE

You gotta hand it to the cowboys. They can turn a birthday cake into a four-alarm fire.

Last summer the Napa Valley (California) County Fair and Rodeo wanted to do something to attract attention to their big PRCA rodeo. Now, I'm not sure how the conversation went at the Fair Board meeting, but maybe something like this . . .

"Why not have a cattle drive down Main Street? Call it the Texas Longhorn Cattle Stampede."

Detractors, stick-in-the-muds, spoilsports, and accountants would have reacted with reasonable objections: "Are you crazy! What if they got loose? You ought to be committed? What if somebody gets hurt? And where on God's green earth could you get anybody who'd let you borrow thirty-three head of full-grown longhorn steers to turn loose on Main Street?"

Into the spotlight stepped Cotton's Rent-A-Cow & Bail Bonds. They assured the city officials that they had steers that were "street-wise and couldn't be spooked and were absolutely controllable" (you can almost hear a cowboy sayin' that, can't you?).

Well, friends, the Texas Longhorn Cattle Stampede made the front page all right. Quotes from onlookers and police included:

"I almost got gored!"

"Not under complete control!"

"Surreal!"

"Unbelievable!"

"We ain't doin' this again!"

"People could have been injured!"

"Cattle riot!"

"Why don't they just load 'em on the truck before someone gets hurt?"

According to the Napa County Sheriff's Posse and local cowboys, it did get a little western. Cattle bolting every which way, clattering against the front door of the Redwood Bank, running through the parking lot, scattering protesters, grazing on the City Hall lawn, snapping side mirrors off parked cars, and lots of screaming.

To put the problem in a nutshell, you could say the steers followed the parade route just a little wider and a littler faster than everyone expected.

The Texas Longhorn Cattle Stampede did what the Fair Board wanted. It drummed up attention for the big rodeo that night. Lots of TV coverage, front page in the paper, and a story that the citizens of Napa will tell for years.

That's good. Although the Fair Board might be a little embarrassed, it's the kind of news story that has thrills and humor and is harmless. And to top it off, it's a cowboy story.

I get the feeling that the Stampede will not become an annual event in Napa, but as one onlooker who'd seen the running of the bulls in Pamplona remarked, "Some people go all the way to Spain to see this sort of thing."

DAVE HOLL '96

*Mama cows are very possessive of their babies. You must exercise
caution if you're going to handle the calf.*

COW ATTACK

"What happened to your pickup seat? Is that buffalo track?"
   "Well, I guess you had to be there. We had a cow attack!"
It all began when me and Roy went out to check the cows.
  *We'd finished lunch and watched our "soap" then forced ourselves
    to rouse.*

  *We's pokin' through the heavy bunch for calves to tag and check
    I spotted one but his ol' mom was bowin' up her neck.*
  *She pawed the ground and swung her head a'slingin' froth and
    spit
    Then bellered like a wounded bull.* "Say, Roy," *I said,* "let's
    quit!"

But Roy was bent on taggin' him and thought to make a grab.
  "Just drive up there beside the calf, I'll pull him in the cab."
*Oh, great. Another stroke of genius, of cowboy derring-do,
  Shornuf, when Roy nabbed the calf, his mama came in too!*

  *And I do mean climbed up in there! Got a foot behind the seat,
    Punched a horn right through the windshield and she wasn't
    very neat.*
  *She was blowin' stuff out both ends till the cab was slick and
    green
    It was on the floor and on the roof and on the calf vaccine.*

If you've been inside a dryer at the local Laundromat
  With a bear and fifty horseshoes then you know just where I's at.
At one point she was sittin' up, just goin' for a ride
  But then she tore the gun rack down. The calf jumped out my
    side.

  I was fightin' with my door lock which she'd smashed a'passin' by
    When she peeked up through the steering wheel and looked me
      in the eye!
  We escaped like paratroopers out the window, landed clear,
    But the cow just kept on drivin' 'cause the truck was still in
      gear.

She topped a hump and disappeared. The blinker light came on
  But if she turned I just can't say, by then the truck was gone.
I looked at Roy. "My truck's a wreck. My coveralls are soaked.
  I'll probably never hear again. I think my ankle's broke.

  "And look at you. Yer pitiful. All crumpled up and stiff
    Like you been eat by wild dogs and pooped over a cliff."
  "But think about it," *Roy said.* "Since Grandpa was alive,
    I b'lieve that that's the firstest time I've seen a cattle drive."

ANTI-SMOKIN' DEVICE

D r. Erfan called to tell me his story. He's spent seventeen years inventing and testing a device to help people quit smoking. It involves a small battery-operated unit that clips in your ear like a hearing aid. Whenever the smoker feels the urge to smoke, he pushes a button on the unit. It sends a micro-amp charge that stimulates a nerve in the ear. In theory, this nerve causes a release of natural body chemicals that reduce the need for a smoke.

Human trials have shown positive results. Enough so that the device is already cleared for use in other countries. But not in the United States. The FDA is not satisfied. They are now demanding animal testing. Thus Dr. Erfan's call. His question: Was I aware of any animals stupid enough to smoke?

Food for thought. First we would have to find a species we could teach to smoke. Then once they were addicted we'd have to teach them to push a button the size of a matchhead whenever they felt the urge.

Certain species, regardless of their stupidity, are eliminated because of lifestyle. Largemouth bass, for instance, whales, or sea anemone could never keep one lit.

Others lack suitable anatomical features necessary for smoking, like prehensile lips—i.e., crocodiles, ducks, or hippopotami.

Or ears in which to insert the unit. Penguins are out, as are frogs, snakes, millipedes, and woodpeckers.

Then the selected species would have to be physically capable of pressing the small button. As you could imagine, even the most dexterous ungulate would have difficulty manipulating its cloven hoof. And I doubt the smartest rhinoceros in the world could reach his ear with his finger.

So, that narrows it down some. I came up with three suggestions for the good doctor. The anteater, the bird dog, and the cowboy.

Even granting the anteater a modicum of intelligence, none of the three species suggested has been known for its good judgment. In addition, all are creatures of habit, work close to the ground, and have a symbiotic relationship with another species that could be helpful in the collusion.

There are some who might question the anteater's ears, but you gotta admit he has smoker's lips!

Dr. Erfan was kind but I could tell he thought my suggestions were ridiculous.

On a flyer I called up Dr. David Kessler, Czar and Mahatma of the FDA, to find out what animals he might suggest that would satisfy their criteria. I understood him to be a crusading anti-smoker and I thought this might be just what the doctor ordered.

But anyone who has dealt with the FDA knows they move with the speed of a glacier. Their motto: "No decision is a good decision."

I'm still waiting for Dr. Kessler to return my call. I can only hope Phillip Morris is on hold, too.

P.S. The FDA eventually responded and justified their reasoning, blaming it on the details. Dr. Erfan is attempting to comply.

HIGH COST OF RECYCLING

We try to be faithful recyclers around our house. I make regular runs to town with the pickup full of newspapers, bottles, aluminum cans, cardboard boxes, and tin. I take old pipe and steel to the scrap metal yard and buy car parts at G & B Salvage.

Yesterday I noticed our toilet paper was labeled *"100% unbleached, 100% recycled paper, 100% post-consumer content and 59.4 square feet in total area."* It's a little like newsprint and I feel odd using toilet paper somebody else has used, but I guess we're doin' the right thing.

Sister Sue said they were using it, too. But it struck her as one of the incongruities of the '90s that recycled toilet paper costs more than a roll of new.

I remember the same thing happened with gasoline when they introduced unleaded. It cost more than regular, to which they had to add the lead.

How 'bout sugarless gum? Bottled water? Egg substitutes? Hamburger Helper costs more per pound than hamburger. Are we being skewered in our noble quest to be green and healthy?

Several years ago the cattle business went on a binge to recycle manure and feed it back to the steers. Concrete pens, elaborate washing systems, dryers, and millions of dollars yielded us a product with the nutrition and palatability of an old mattress for the price of caviar.

The trend toward lean beef gives me second thoughts, as well. Just looking at a hubcap-size Holstein round steak, you realize God intended it for taco meat. But if that same steak goes into a specialty health food meat counter it costs twice as much. It is labeled "Au Bouf Delite" and is guaranteed to contain less than .01 percent fat. Cooking instructions are explicit: Boil for three days and pound until flat as hammered gravy.

My mother saved and reused tinfoil, wax paper, jelly glasses, bacon fat, soup bones, old bananas, cloth diapers, baby clothes, string, ribbon, wrapping paper, and cottage cheese containers. There are still those around who straighten and reuse old nails, buckets of bolts, fence wire, and lumber.

Maybe, in truth, if you counted the labor, it costs more to straighten old nails than to buy new ones. But thriftiness forced recycling.

Today, the high cost of recycled, sugarless, lean, unleaded products is the price we pay to do our part in makin' the world a better place.

So when pondering the use of environmentally correct antique toilet paper we can envision the historical significance and gain some satisfaction knowing this same paper might have been used by Davy Crockett, Oprah Winfrey, or Chief Sitting Bull. And if that don't make it worth the price I'll send you some slightly used corncobs.

Another true story.

IN THE DOGHOUSE

It's not easy being a missionary distributing religious pamphlets door-to-door. Homeowners will go to extremes to avoid listening to you.

Audrey and her husband, Walter, have a ranch in British Columbia around Fraser Lake. They are cattle people and run the place pretty much by themselves.

Walter had gone out to check the cows one morning. After doin' breakfast dishes, Audrey headed out to the shop to get somethin'. Midway she was surprised by a sneeze. It dislodged her upper plate and it hit the gravel six feet away.

In the time it took her to blink, her new pup, Daisy, raced in, scooped up the dentures, and was off like a shot.

"Here, Daisy . . . here. Daisy . . . good dog . . . yer a good puppy . . . give Mama her teeth. Come, Daisy . . . sit . . . stay . . . Daisy! Come here, you miserable little excuse for a mongrel's offspring. You paper-eatin', cat-chasin', slipper-chewin', sorry, no-good . . . Here, Daisy. No! No! Git over here before I pound you into wolf chow!"

Daisy and the old dog, Blue, were makin' big circles in the yard with Audrey hot on their heels alternately coaxing and cussing the canine teeth thief.

Daisy dropped the teeth. Just as Audrey dove for the slobbery dentures, Blue swooped in and scooped 'em up. Out into the driveway the three of them raced. Back and forth between the shop and the garden fence.

"Blue, come here. Whoa, Blue . . . drop those teeth or you'll be bear bait! Come on, Blue . . ."

Blue smiled at her. He looked like Miss America.

Then he dropped the teeth, but Daisy intercepted before Audrey could make her move.

Daisy raced to the doghouse, situated by the back door porch, and dived in. Audrey followed till she was waist-deep in the doghouse and wrestled the precious dentures from Daisy.

Just as she started to back out she heard gravel crunch and a car door slam. Footsteps tromped up to the back door.

The voices of two women were introducing themselves and asking Audrey personal questions about her religion. Actually they were talking to Audrey's protruding backside. Audrey had her teeth in her hand. They were slippery, sticky, and covered with dirt. She had a short conversation from inside the doghouse and very quickly the ladies departed.

As Audrey breathed a sigh of relief she heard one of the ladies say, "You know, some people will go to any lengths . . ."

The continuing decline in the number of family farms seems to elicit transitory concern among politicians and national media. However, there are many reasons for this decline. This is only one.

INHERITING THE FAMILY FARM

The latest statistics show that less than 2 percent of the population is directly involved in production agriculture. It is a function of an increasing population and a limited amount of farm ground. Technology is able to keep up, so that less bodies are required to produce an ever-increasing cornucopia of food and fiber.

But on a personal level the story isn't quite so simple.

Tom was raised on a dairy farm in the Great Lakes region: three hundred cows, nine hundred acres. His grandfather established the farm and passed it down to Tom's father.

Tom's childhood memories are of work. By the time his mother came in to wake him and his two brothers for school, she and Dad had already finished the morning milking. By nine years of age he was already part of the family farm. Until he was old enough to milk he pushed cows to the barn, fed calves, forked silage, and did whatever kids do, which was plenty.

High school activities like dances, meetings, sports, and girls all hinged around milking time and chores. He didn't need to work at McDonald's during summer vacation. If he wanted work there was plenty at home.

He went to college. His two brothers left to work elsewhere. Now Tom is thirty-three, married with kids, and has a good job at the local Co-op. Dad has been using hired labor since the boys left, but Dad is getting older.

Tom makes his daily rounds, does his job, and is active in the community. But hovering over everything he does is that niggling feeling that maybe he should go back to the farm.

After all, it is a showplace. The result of uncountable man-hours and love and sweat poured into it by two generations preceding him. It made him the good man that he is. And he could run it well if he chose to. Guilt rides him like the winter fog off Lake Michigan.

In my opinion Tom need not feel guilty. Nor should his parents place that onus upon the shoulders of their inheritors. Each person has his or her own calling.

But I would suggest that there are many with no inheritance who would leap at the chance to own a farm. Immigrants, hired men, college grads, feed salesmen, and pencil-pushin' farm boys whose dream is to work their own place.

It would be ideal if both the parents and their kids could cooperate to actively seek out those potential pardners and integrate them into the operation. With the idea they could eventually buy it out. It would be to everyone's relief and good for the continuing productivity of the farm. In other words, take 'em into the family.

To farm you must love the land. That's the only reason I can think of that explains why farming is an occupation where labor is never counted as a business expense.

Another illustration of the chasm that separates city and country.
And, of course, I didn't make this up—although I changed the name
of the cookie store and Ralph . . . and I Baxterized it a little.

THE LOST CHICKEN

Lynne parked her car in the little lot behind Cookies Du Moi. It was an odd little corner of Salt Lake City mixing pawn-shops with barred windows, liquor stores, and an invasion of upscale pastel-colored urban grazing and knickknack shops. Small stores with cute names offering yogurt, dried flowers in a basket, ducks wearing bonnets, and specialty bagels that cost more than a five-pound pot roast. New Age music drifted into the street.

Lynne noticed a shabbily dressed man working his way around the parked cars, peering in windows and under bumpers. She locked her car and entered Cookies Du Moi.

"There's a man out in the parking lot acting suspicious. He might be trying to break into a car," reported Lynne.

The lady behind the counter was casually dressed, but brand names emblazoned her persona. "Yes," she said, "he's one of the locals. He's doing a favor for the owner of Raphael's Wreaths and Incense Boutique next door. See, Ralph, I mean Raphael, brought his pickup to work this morning but he forgot that a hen had been nesting in the back. The hen jumped out after he parked. I think that man is looking for it."

"He'll have a little stew tonight, I'll bet," chuckled Lynne.

"Oh, no . . . he'll give it back."

"I doubt it. He looked like he could use a good meal."

"Well," replied the proprietress of Cookies Du Moi, "I'd give it back if I caught it. Wouldn't you?"

"Personally, I don't think I'd spend much time tryin' to track an escaped chicken through this neighborhood," said Lynne, still joking.

"Yes, but if she isn't caught she'll be lost in the city," said the lady with mild indignation.

"It's just a chicken," observed Lynne.

"But she was kind of a pretty chicken. I'm worried for her."

Lynne, who had been around the barnyard, said, "Well, maybe she'll wander into Colonel Sanders' Shelter for Homeless Chickens."

"I sense you are not taking the chicken's problem seriously."

"I came in here to get cookies."

After sacking her order, the cookie lady said, "I'm really concerned about your lack of compassion. Chickens have feelings. What if you were nesting in the back of a pickup, got hauled to a strange city, and got lost?"

"You've got a point," sighed Lynne. "Let's see if we can get the chicken a lawyer and sue Raphael."

P.S. A year after this commentary ran, I met a cosmetologist from Salt Lake City who had captured a chicken in her neighborhood. She had heard the commentary on NPR and made the connection. We had a good visit, but I forgot to ask the eventual disposition of the chicken.

One of my favorite poems and sort of autobiographical.

WORKIN' FOR WAGES

I've worked fer wages all my life
    watchin' other people's stock
And the outfits I hired on to
    didn't make you punch a clock.

Let you work until you finished!
    Like the feedlots in the fall,
When they'd roll them calves in on ya
    they'd jis' walk the fence and bawl.

We'd check the pens and pull the sick
    and push and treat and ride
Then process new arrivals
    that kept comin' like the tide.

And I've calved a lotta heifers
    though it's miserable sometimes,
It's somethin' that I'm good at
    and it's like she's sorta mine.

She knows I ain't the owner
    but we're not into protocol.
She's a cow and I'm a cowboy
    and I guess that says it all. . . .

Got no truck with politicians
    who whine and criticize
'Bout corporate agribusiness,
    I guess they don't realize

Somebody's gotta own 'em
that can pay the entry fee.
Why, who they think puts up the dough
to hire ol' boys like me?

Oh, I bought a set of heifers once
maybe fifteen years ago.
I held 'em through a calvin'
then I had to let 'em go

'Cause all I did was worry
'bout how to pay the bills.
Took the fun outta cow punchin',
I don't need them kinda thrills.

Though I wouldn't mind a'ownin' me
a little hideaway
So when some outfit laid me off
I'd have a place to stay.

But I figger I'm jis' lucky
to be satisfied at heart
That I'm doin' what I'm good at
and I'm playin' a small part

In a world that's complicated,
where the bosses fight it out
With computers and consultants
and their counterparts with clout.

They're so busy bein' bosses
they've no time to spare, somehow,
So they have to hire someone like me
to go out and punch their cow.

A great story . . . but if it sounds familiar, read the following commentary, as well.

MINNESOTA OREOS

It's a long way from the country to the city. Not by miles necessarily, but by state of mind.

Matt was a cowboy, even though he lived in the heart of Minnesota, where natives consider cowboys as suspect as Republicans or Southern Baptists. He owned a horse, wore a cowboy hat, and spoke in an odd drawl.

His nephew was stationed at the North Lakes Naval Facility near Chicago. This nephew had pestered Uncle Matt to take a day off and visit him. He even suggested Matt take the commuter train from Minneapolis. Matt was finally convinced.

He found the embarking point for the train and boarded. At the first stopover all passengers were allowed to disembark at the station for twenty minutes.

Matt climbed off, taking his ticket with him. Wearing his cowboy hat, boots, and duster, he wandered inside. He stood in line at the snack bar and bought a box of milk and a six-pack of Oreo cookies.

He sat down at one of the tables next to a businessman. The businessman wore a tie and was reading the *Wall Street Journal* through half glasses balanced on his nose. Matt thought he looked like Ward Cleaver.

Matt opened his milk, took a swig, and opened the cookies. The businessman glanced at Matt, then took one of the cookies.

Matt looked up at Ward, who'd gone back to reading, munching on the cookie. Matt ate a cookie himself. As he washed it down, Ward reached out and snared another cookie.

People in Minnesota are trained not to make others ill at ease, so Matt didn't say anything. But he wondered if this was now acceptable behavior inside the castle walls of Minneapolis/St. Paul. Part of some inspired welfare decree for those who had no cookies. He did take a second cookie, though, and quickly stuffed a third in his mouth.

Like a striking snake Ward Cleaver grabbed the last cookie! He scarfed it, stood up in a huff and stalked off.

Matt obviously had offended him. Matt wondered if he would later be turned in to the Social Services Police. "Ah, well," he thought. "It ain't this way in the country. Nobody'd take even one cookie without askin', and to top it off the freeloader never said thanks!"

Matt got up to board the train, picked up the wrapper, and tossed it in the trash. He felt in his pocket for his ticket and there were his Oreo cookies.

It is every commentator's concern that he may inadvertently give credit to the wrong reference, misquote some famous passage, or be accused of plagiary. I got caught, innocent though my intentions, and taken to task for passing along a harmless, funny story that had been told before.

This commentary followed hot on the heels of my mistake.

OREOS APOLOGY

Great Scott! Now I know how Homer felt when he named his epic poem about the return of Ulysses *The Hitchhiker's Guide to the Galaxy.* His P-mail (parchment mail) overflowed and Mercury wore the wings right off his Nikes delivering messages from irate fans of one Douglas Adams, who had already used that title. So Homer, in contrition, just called it *The Odyssey.*

Yes, friends, I too have been the recipient of indignant P-mail, E-mail, and junk mail from defenders of that selfsame author of Homeric proportions—i.e., Douglas Adams.

You see, in my last commentary I told a story related to me by a friend in western Minnesota (an unexplored territory not unlike northern Greenland or southern New Jersey). The story involved Oreo cookies. Unbeknownst to my friend or myself, a similar story appeared in the book *So Long and Thanks for All the Fish,* by none other than that same Douglas Adams.

I was horror struck! The producers at NPR were already boiling the oil and sharpening their cat-o'-nine-tails when they called with the news. "One should never assume," they chastened, "that regular listeners to public radio, regardless of their generosity to a fault, their tolerance of commentators who talk funny and compassion for obscure practitioners of the folk arts, would let go by such an egregious faux pas as you have made!"

"What can I do to make it right?" I cried out. Put a warning on all my poems like the cigarette people, take out a full-page ad in the *New York Times,* do two years of community service like Leona Helmsley and Saddam Hussein?

Too ashamed to call Mr. Adams, I've been wallowing in my sweat lodge waiting for a vision. It came to me that a simple sincere apology to Douglas Adams and all his Adamites would be best.

So from the bottom of my sackcloth and ashes I beg forgiveness and express my regrets for any anxiety I've caused.

OFF MIKE—So, ya think that'll work? Listen, I've got a great idea for another commentary. It's about this little cowboy who tells a lie and his nose gets longer each time. The guy that told me the story raises crickets . . .

The two characters in this story are as real as creaks in a new saddle. They are both top hands, good cowboys, family men, and lifetime friends. It was my good fortune to work with them during my ten years as the company vet for the Simplot Livestock Company in the northwest. Although they dickered and played tricks on one another, they were close as a pair of dice in a crapshooter's hand.

LEROY AND TOM

Everybody has a Christmas that stands out in their memory like dandruff on Superman's cape. Mine was several years ago. Bah Humbug Bill, the cow buyer, made a deal on a set of cows down below Snowville, Utah. Leroy, Tom, and I were to go down, work 'em, and ship 'em back home. Bah Humbug set it up for December 23rd. He, of course, would not be able to be there to help.

Leroy and Tom were both members of the Owyhee County Sheriff's Possum. We borrowed Albert's new blue pickup and headed out. Leroy was raised down in the country where we were goin'. He was driving and took a few shortcuts. We were on a side road going toward Strevell and Leroy had ol' Blue kicked up to eighty-five miles an hour. We cautioned him about speeding.

"No sweat," he said. "The police have never patrolled this ol' road."

Ten minutes later red and blue flashing lights reflected in the rearview mirror.

"Snowplow?" asked Tom.

Leroy pulled over and stomped back to the state patrol car. He returned, started up, and drove on in silence.

"Did you show him yer deputy sheriff's badge, Leroy?" we asked. "Yeah," he said, "I told 'em I was takin' these two lunatics to the asylum down south. One of 'em thinks he's a vetinary and the other thinks he's a cowboy!"

The ticket cost him forty-five dollars.

Leroy suggested I buy the gas and he'd buy us dinner at the finest restaurant in Tremonton. He asked Tom to pick up the motel bill and promised he'd treat us to a meal fit for a king! We cleaned up and went with him to supper. We were in a festive mood. Holly and Christmas music were everywhere. The café even had its own Santa who gave candy to the kids.

"Git anything you want, boys," Leroy encouraged us. "It's on me!" We ordered steak and lobster with all the trimmings and polished off a mince pie. Santa came over and gave us candy. We thanked Leroy for his generosity.

"Check please," he said, smiling and picking his teeth. He patted his pocket confidently. Then he patted his other hip pocket. Then his front pocket and his shirt. He ransacked his coat pockets. He looked up with desperation on his face. "I forgot my wallet!"

Next mornin' on the way out to the ranch we stopped for clipper blades. Tom bought a new pair of blue handyman gloves with little white speckles on them.

At the ranch Leroy was mouthin' and puttin' in Ritchey ear tags; bloody work. I was pregnancy checkin'; messy work. Tom was brandin', but he was still wearin' his old yellow gloves with holes in the fingers. He was savin' his new ones, he claimed. I slipped over to the pickup and found his new ones. I put on the left one and gave the right to Leroy. After working an hour Tom noticed my left hand.

"I've got gloves just like that. Only mine aren't covered with cow manure," he said. He noticed Leroy's gloved right hand, which was caked with blood. The light slowly dawned. "I quit!" he said. It was the third time he'd quit since eight-thirty that morning.

I never worried. Those two fellers had the perfect arrangement; nobody else would work for Leroy and nobody else would hire Tom.

Merry Christmas to y'all, especially you, Leroy and Tom!

It should come as no surprise that I can't cook. Furthermore, I'm not a very discriminating diner. Matter of fact, the fajitas in this piece actually sound good.

COWBOY VEGETARIAN COOKBOOK

When beef gets short a lot of cowboys are forced to do without. The cook must come up with meatless meals. The following recipes are from the *Cowboy Vegetarian Cookbook.*

Tennis Shoe Tongue: Select an old one. The price is better and it may have picked up some natural flavor depending on where it has been worn. Boiling is suggested, but it may also be fried to a crisp and served on a bed of marinated sweatshirt. Garnish with pickled shoestring.

Seed Corn Cap Pizza: Carefully clean with a fish-scaling knife. Remove all metal buttons, rivets, and any plastic tabs. Flatten the cap by soaking in linseed oil, then placing it underneath a doormat that gets heavy use. Once pliable, cover it with lots of cheese and ketchup. Dry kibbles or dust motes may be sprinkled as a topping for variety.

Fan Belt Fajitas: The most succulent fan belts can be found on old farm equipment moldering in your boneyard. It should be sliced into bite-sized chunks. Tenderize before cooking by soaking in fingernail polish remover. Fry in lard along with half a hatful of three-quarter-inch black plastic hose and shredded playing cards. Serve with beer and jalapeños. It tastes a lot like abalone.

Rawhide Stew: Ever wondered what to do with those old reins, quirts, or saddle tree bark? This recipe has been tried and tested from ancient Mongolians right up through Donner Pass. Place the strips of rawhide in a pot and boil for as many weeks as the firewood holds out. What you add to the stew depends on what's available—i.e., pinecones, hoof trimmings, iron pyrite, or old hat brims. It's filling but don't expect much more.

Roasted Kak: Ever eat a saddle? Some parts are edible. Dig a hole big enough to bury a small mule. Burn elm, cottonwood, and old tires to get a bed of coals. Wrap the saddle in a plastic tarp (blue), place it on the coals, and cover with dirt. Cook for hours on end. Dig up and serve with baked faucet washers. Feeds up to two truckloads of hungry cowboys.

That should give you an idea of what you can do when you run out of beef at the ranch. There are many other cowboy vegetarian recipes, like Latigo Jerky, Gunstock Pâté, and Smokin' Joe's Copenhagen Torte, but this should get you started.

The product of high cerebral RPM's in neutral.

NOAH'S DISPERSAL SALE

PUBLIC NOTICE

To: Residents of Mt. Ararat School District
Ref: Noah, visionary and livestock hauler, recently returned from an exotic cruise, will be holding his first après cruise yard sale. Many items will be offered to tickle your nautical or agricultural fancy. All sales final, not guaranteed against mildew.
Included in the sale:

- approximately 2,400 cages (wire, wicker, horsehair, iron, rope, screen, etc.)
- lots of salt blocks. (Actually, it was Lot's wife who was turned into the first salt block)
- adjustable nose tongs (fits both water buffalo, hippo, and elephant)
- 1.2 million species of insects still frozen in a quart jar (could be used as parakeet feed or turned loose on the world)
- two cans of Off
- one rhino twitch
- a mastodon fur coat (soon to be listed as endangered)
- set of teeth floats for small rodents
- dried poultry waste, including pigeon, pelican, buzzard, banty, canary, and condor
- hoof nippers (fits any species from emu to gnu)
- box of assorted pills, including wildcat suppositories, camel antacid boli, Dramamine, and Nyquil for bears
- two hog snares (will double as calving tool and snake catcher)
- two life jackets for small mammals, size prairie dog to porcupine

- crocodile balling gun
- anteater tongue depressors
- giraffe stomach hose
- Small library containing:

    How to Get Ahead in the New World Even Though Fish Have a Head Start

    Practical Uses of Animal Waste—from Caulking and Rudder Grease to Fertilizer and Finger Painting

    How to Survive 40 Days and 40 Nights Cooped Up with a Man Who Keeps Saying, "Pretty Good Ark, Ey, Mother?"

    The Illustrated Guide to Sexing Amphibians, Newts, and Domestic Fowl

    Noah's Captain's Log, entitled, *One More Day Like This and I'll Never Get the Corn In*

- and finally: firewood (gopher) by the cubit

Garrison Keillor is not the only proponent of duct tape.

DUCT TAPE IN AGRICULTURE

A collection of testimonials for duct tape in agriculture . . .

From B.A., large animal vet:

I've been a duct tape believer ever since I had a cow tear her bag on a bob wire fence. It was a ghastly gash. She was in pain and frightened. There was no way I could close the wound until . . . I began wrapping her with duct tape! I began just behind the elbow and started circling her girth, then her ribs and her flanks with duct tape. I eventually was able to wrap the bag, leaving the four teats and tail poking out. Six months later the tape fell off and she was cured!

From F.W., horseshoer:

One afternoon I had been called to shoe a miniature horse. I was expecting one in the St. Bernard–Great Dane class, but this one was not much bigger than a medium house cat. I built to the task and was bent over the left hind leg when my nipper slipped. I had accidentally trimmed the hoof clear off at the hock. I panicked until . . . I remembered the roll of duct tape I always keep in my watch pocket. Using two ¼-inch × 1-inch bolts, I splinted the leg back together and wrapped it with duct tape. Each week I added another twelve to fifteen feet of duct tape. Two months later it seems to be working, although he's still walking funny.

From D.W., poultry pathologist:

Doing surgery on chickens is uncommon. Whenever I saw a chicken he was usually dead. And yet many suffered from ingrown feathers. Most polloqueros (chicken cowboys from Mexico) spent hours each day gently plucking the ingrown feathers from afflicted hens. One afternoon I was helping and happened to drop a chicken on a strip of duct tape I had circled around my feet to stave off fire ants. When I picked up the chicken her brisket was plucked clean. Inspired, the polloqueros completely wrapped me with duct tape, sticky side out, and slapped the chicken's afflicted area containing the ingrown feather against my body. This technique has since been adopted to declaw cats and in beauty shops as a depilatory.

From Y.K., team roper:

I used to carry rawhide, latigo, hole punchers, awls, Chicago screws, harness buckles, rubber wraps, bell boots, Super Glue, baby powder, rivets, snaps, curb chains, and fencing pliers in my emergency box. Now all I carry is duct tape. I've used it to repair broken cinches, lengthen reins, rebuild hondos, plait manes, wrap horns, tie on, dress wounds, plug bloody noses, and replace thumbs. I now wear chinks made out of duct tape, have padded my saddle with duct tape and braided a nice hatband with duct tape.

Today I have covered my pickup with duct tape and written "Born to Rope" in duct tape on the side of my trailer. I'm ready and lookin' for a pardner. Just call 1-800-DukTap.

Sometimes inspiration falls from the sky. Bob and Nina are success-
ful purebred cattle raisers in Washington State and his original idea
was the seed from whence this commentary sprang.

COW POLYGAMY

I was visiting with Nina after their bull sale this spring. She remarked on the overabundance of bulls for sale around the country this year. Competition is stiff. She said she had counted the number of bulls advertised in the livestock paper and figgered if they were placed end to end they would reach farther than you could point.

Her husband, Bob, ever the deep thinker, pondered on the dilemma and came up with the perfect modern '90s answer: outlaw polygamy in cows.

"By gosh," I thought, "a solution that fits the times. One bull per cow." But then I began to think it through.

Would each cowyage (as opposed to marriage in horses) be intended for life? Or would we allow for divorce and recowyage (or dehorse and remarriage)?

Would a cowyaged pair be allowed to mingle with other cowyaged couples in the pasture? Could both the bull and the cow be trusted to ignore the lip curling, tail rubbing, and perfume of others? Would they stoically pay no attention if sidled up to and mounted by a less-disciplined member of their community?

Or would each couple be fenced in a small enclosure loosely based on a suburban housing development? One where each morning the bull would be driven to an eight-to-five field with other bulls to spend the day grazing and grumbling about the rancher, the bullfights in Mexico City, and how alfalfa ain't what it used to be?

Would the cows, likewise, drop their calf off at day care and go to their respective cow field, where they'd eat grass, talk about their calves, and share fantasies about bull pictures in the Artificial Insemination calendar?

Would cowyages be arranged or would courtship be allowed? Would chaperones be required at the weaning prom?

If a bull was caught posing as a molasses salesman and making unwanted advances at the housecow, would he be hamburger at sunrise?

After considerable rumination I have concluded that trying to work out the details of outlawing polygamy in cows might put an end to it before it began. Even if we passed the law, the plan would probably fail anyway. Cows have never felt guilty about practicing polygamy in the first place. And no amount of political correctness training or moral browbeating would make these now-consenting polygamists consider asking that basic question. The one that separates cowkind from mankind . . . "I know you love me, but will you respect me next estrus?"

Although I don't claim to be a farrier, I do shoe my own horses. Veterinarians and horseshoers have a lot in common. We're both walking up to a strange horse, who outweighs us considerably, and at the very least we're going to make him uncomfortable—or worse, cause him some pain. Horses can sense this.

SHOEIN' PIGEYE

"Just count me out," *said Wilford as he lay there in the dirt,*
  A shoein' rasp behind his ear, a hoof print on his shirt.
"I'll handle this," *said Freddie.* "You jus' git outta the way.
  This sorry bag of buzzard bait has met his match today."

The horse weren't much to look at, just the kind a trader'd buy
  But you knew that he was trouble when you looked him in the eye.
It was small and mean and glittered, as deep as Jacob's well,
  Like lookin' down the smokestack of the furnace room in Hell.

Freddie grabbed a set of nippers and bent to grab a hoof.
  When he woke up . . . his shoein' chaps were danglin' from the roof.
His shirttail hung in tatters and his watch had come unwound.
  The nipper's orbit finally peaked. They clattered to the ground.

"You get a twitch," *said Freddie,* "I'm about to clean his clock."
  He tied a rope around his neck and fished it past the hock
Then pulled back on the sideline to instill a little fear
  When Pigeye bit a good-sized chunk from Wilford's offside ear.

245

Wilford tangled in the sideline and tried to navigate
Whilst draggin' 'round the horse corral like alligator bait.
Freddie tried to stop this trollin' with a loop around the head,
And it might'a worked if Freddie'd only roped the horse instead.

But, of course, he caught pore Wilford, who left a funny track . . .
Sorta like an oil slick, when Freddie jerked the slack.
By now the boys were testy and tired of this travail
They figgered they'd be done by noon but they'd not drove a
nail.

"Go git the boss's Humvee. We'll winch him to a post."
They got the cayuse necked up tight, and set to work . . . almost
'Cause the halter broke and Pigeye walked the length of Freddie's
back.
They rolled beneath the axle like two lovers in a sack.

Freddie heard the sound of gunfire like a thousand amplifiers,
"I've got the sucker pinned down, Fred, I shot out all the
tires!"
It was dark when Wilford stood up and laid his hammer down.
A gross of crooked horseshoe nails lay scattered all around.

The place looked like a cross between the tomb of Gen'ral Grant
And a Puppy Chow explosion at the Alpo dog food plant!
Wilford couldn't move his elbow but he grinned and proudly said,
"Ol pard, we done a good day's work," to what was left of Fred.

Freddie crawled out from the wreckage
and staggered to one knee,
"What say we wait till mornin'
to put on the other three . . .?"

Rarely do my commentaries make observations on current events. That's the purview of the regular Morning Edition *crew. However, during the brouhaha over making nature films, I couldn't pass it up.*

NATURE FILMS

Here we are friends, on the Serengeti Plains in the wilds of Serengeti." As the crowd leans in closer to the television we see the swaying boab trees . . . an endless sea of grass waving off into the horizon. We hear the quiet buzz of tsetse flies humming strains of "Baby Elephant Walk." Just as we are becoming mesmerized into the peaceful surroundings on the screen, a lone gazelle suddenly bursts on the scene.

It leaps and dives, graceful arcs, nimble footwork, darting back and forth like a cockroach wearing cleats. Then, out of the savannah, like a big shoe, streaks the jungle's answer to Michael Jordan, Charlie the Cheetah! Charlie pounces on the gazelle and drags him to the ground.

Another example of nature's survival of the fittest. But did you ever wonder how the film crew happened to be there at that exact moment?

As you may have read, nature programs are under close scrutiny this spring. One of the most popular is the subject of an exposé. It accuses the producer of staging scenes, of using tame animals or zoo animals, and of staking out "prey" for the predators to pounce on.

But may I point out to those who are shocked by this accusation, this is television. Movies. Show business. The media of revisionist history, docudrama, infomercials, and the Home Shopping Network. A business where the facts are altered and endings changed to make a more entertaining program.

Wanton acts of animal cruelty are to be avoided. But filming an anteater licking the inside of a termite mound from the termite's point of view takes a little more planning. I mean, how long can a cameraman wait inside a termite's living room?

Anybody who ever tried to get a dog or kid to repeat a trick while you run and get the camera knows how hard it is to film spontaneous acts.

I've always assumed nature films were staged. I figured the crew gathered after breakfast and drove to a carefully selected spot. They arrive when the lighting is just right.

From the back of a used stock truck (with Nairobi plates) they unload an old antelope, a gnu with footrot and six crippled rabbits. The director points to the truck driver and the prey limps out.

Then the director points to the animal trainer. He releases his leopard. Cameras roll . . . the leopard bounds toward the hobbling gnu, leaps for his throat, and throws him to the ground.

"Cut!" cries the director.

The leopard helps the gnu up, dusts him off, and they go back to the truck. Everybody packs up and gets back to the hotel by cocktail time.

Isn't that how they filmed *Jurassic Park*?

The request . . .

NATIONAL PUBLIC RADIO

TO: Baxter Black
FR: Charlotte Taylor
DT: September 28, 1993

Promotion and Public Affairs is collecting short essays from
NPR staff and commentators talking about things that they do
especially well. These "How They Do It" essays will be used in a
staff/station newsletter we're about to launch; stations will also
use them in program guides and local newspaper pitches.

    If you can spare a few minutes, we'd like you to pen a few
paragraphs, serious or funny, about something you think you
do well (related to your work outside of NPR, or to your radio
essays). . . .

My response . . .

THE HOULIHAN

How many times have you found yourself in the middle of a
cavvy of horses? They are thundering around you like a
school of tuna circling a drain. You have selected a wild-
eyed piebald with rollers in his nostrils who manages to stay to the
outside as they race around inside the round corral. He immediately knows you want him, and he is doing his best to evade cap-
ture. Swinging a flat loop is dang near impossible what with all the
heads poking up, so you instigate your plan by employing the
houlihan.

    Being right-handed and in the Northern Hemisphere, you start
them circling clockwise. You build a good-sized loop, flop it over

your left shoulder, palm down, and wait. The object is to throw a loop that is vertical like a rolling tire and letting the chosen horse run into it headfirst.

By easing closer to the circling bunch you slow them down and let them slip through the bottleneck till the horse you want is in the lead. Then you swing your loop back to your right, palm up, thumb pointing backward, and with one smooth gesture, always keeping your palm away from you, you rotate your wrist and throw the loop in front of the galloping horse. At the conclusion of the throw your arm should be extended, your palm out, fingers spread and thumb pointing down.

After approximately fourscore and ten attempts and catching the wrong horse seventeen times, you should have mastered the houlihan and caught the piebald.

If you are left-handed, hold this page up to a mirror and follow the same instructions.

CAUTION: Throwing the houlihan is not recommended in a locker room full of NBA all-stars or an embassy reception near the hors d'oeuvres table.

Farmers and ranchers are very aware of sensational headlines regarding the food they produce—i.e., HORMONES IN BEEF, ALAR IN APPLES, SALMONELLA IN CANTALOUPES. Before the public became jaded toward the sky-is-falling press reporting, a single headline could destroy the market for a producer's perishable goods.

The market can also be affected by more subtle means.

BABE

This year the movie *Babe* was nominated for several Academy Awards, including Best Picture. It was very popular and made a lot of money. It stars a pig named Babe. A gilt, to be more specific . . . a feeder pig maybe weighin' eighty to one hundred pounds. But it was a cute pig. It talked, of course; was kind and brave. And to top it off, it did heroic deeds and yet maintained a sensitivity that would make Phil Donahue blush.

All this anthropomorphism, giving a pig human qualities, is necessary if moviemakers expect an audience to relate to the hero. It made me wonder if the movie *Babe* had a deleterious effect on the price of the Other White Meat. I made a couple calls, but the pork producers were noncommittal. They had an up market this spring.

But I would not have been surprised if it had. The sheep and veal people have known for years that it is hard to convince the public to eat something cute.

Rabbit raisers are careful to avoid any advertising including the words *BunnyBurger* or *BBQ'd Bunny Ribs* or *Bunny on a Grill.* Even in the frozen north they've never developed a market for the Baby Seal Club Sandwich. Australians have never had trouble eating lamb, mostly because they're so numerous over there they are thought of more often as ants or roadkill. Yet in my one trip Down Under I saw no Koala Kabobs. Too cute.

The Chinese seem to eat anything under the sun, from thousand-year-old eggs to objects that crawl on the seafloor, but I've never heard of a Panda Patty.

The reverse is also true . . . that it is easier to eat something less cuddly. That may be part of the success of the chicken business. In books, movies, and stories, chickens are seldom portrayed in flattering roles. They're usually stupid or pompous—i.e., Foghorn Leghorn; Chicken Little; Huey, Dewey, and Louie. Even the Little Red Hen turns out to be a Republican.

But I do suspect the pork producers were worried about their business while *Babe* was showing in thousands of theaters to hundreds of thousands of young impressionable kids. Had to be. I know French restauranteurs worried when *The Black Stallion* was showing.

BOB BLACK

RELIGIOUS REFLECTIONS

I was sittin' in the back row of a beautiful little church in a
mountain town in the Rockies. I was there for the wedding of
the daughter of good friends.

As the service progressed, my attention was drawn to a banner
that hung on the wall. It was handmade, cut from cloth, and
intended to be inspiring. It read MOUNT UP WITH WINOS.

Many thoughts went through my mind as I tried to absorb the
full meaning of this elaborate banner. I had come to realize over
the years that many Protestant churches have become more liberal in their teachings.

Acceptance of alternative lifestyles, less moralizing, less blatant
emphasis on money, more convenient schedules, and greater tolerance of lesser sins—i.e., fall football, alcohol, sex, and non-
Christian religions.

And there is something to be said for that religious creed—after
all, Jesus himself never discriminated.

Bein' a thinker myself, I began to concoct other potential banner
slogans that might be acceptable in this New Age congregation:
RIDE WITH THE RISQUÉ, LIE DOWN WITH THE LITIGIOUS, COMMUNE
WITH THE IMMORAL, DO LUNCH WITH THE CHARACTER DEPRIVED.

The wedding audience was mostly ranch people, men with sun-
burned faces wearin' new jeans and uncomfortable in their ties.
The women wore their best dresses, and the kids were glad to be
anywhere off the ranch.

I'd come with my family to pay tribute to the parents . . . my
friends. But I admit my distraction with the banner had consumed
a good part of my attention during the service. I began to think
that it was inappropriate.

When the soloist rose and sang the final George Strait love song
while the bride and groom escaped, she was positioned right
below the banner. Poor planning, I thought, or at least in poor
taste.

As we were filing out I asked my daughter what she thought of the banner.

"Which one?" she asked.

"The one right above the singer," I answered.

She studied it and read aloud, "Mount Up with Wings. Kinda cool, I guess. Why?"

"Oh," I said, vowing silently to start wearing my glasses, "just curious."

One of the more profound observations I made after becoming a commentator was that you gotta be careful. There are people out there who believe what you say.

This piece stimulated a healthy pile of requests for copies often prefaced by "I enjoy yer funny stuff, but this one . . ."

JUST WORDS

They were just words:

"*Tear down the Berlin Wall!*" Reagan to Gorbachev at the Brandenburg Gate, 1987.

"*Chance of rain.*" Weatherman in Iowa during the '93 flood.

"*Give me liberty or give me death.*" Patrick Henry, 1775.

"*I wish I'd never read this book . . . so I could read it again for the first time.*" Dan Trimble about Hemingway's *Old Man and the Sea*, 1992.

"*The Grass Is Always Greener over the Septic Tank.*" Erma Bombeck, 1976.

We often underestimate the value of words. "*Good job, son.*" "*Best cobbler I ever ate.*" "*Did you paint that yourself?*" "*I'm really proud of you.*" "*Thank ya, love.*"

We underestimate their power. "*You shouldn't'a let that kid beat ya.*" "*Maybe you should lose some weight, Hon.*" "*You should'a tried harder.*" "*Not again; they've heard those stories before.*" "*You do that every time!*"

There are people whose opinions we truly value. There are people whose praise we'd die for. They are often two different things. Sometimes we genuinely would like to improve ourselves. "*Yer lettin' your rope go too soon.*" "*Give him his head.*" "*Always check the hind feet when you set him up.*"

Sometimes we just need encouragement. *"You did the best you could." "You looked like you won from where I sat." "It sure runs better after you worked on it."*

Most everyone is the most important person in someone's life. It is no small responsibility. It should be a crime if we don't realize and recognize that importance, because what you say can have such long-lasting effect:

"I believe you got the makin's of a world champion." Ty Murray's mom.

"I know you can do it, but be careful." James A. Lovell, Jr.'s wife.

"Believe in yourself." Martin Luther King's Sunday School teacher.

"Ask not what your country can do for you, but what you can do for your country." JFK.

"Write about what you know." My college English professor after giving me an F on a poem I wrote for a class assignment.

"You'll never amount to anything." Too many of us, too many times.

Words . . . like burrs under a blanket, like nails in a coffin.

Like a single match in a sea of gasoline.

HERE COME DE JUDGE

I make it a rule never to be a judge of livestock, gymnastics, county fairs, or rodeo queens. I made an exception. The Colorado Department of Agriculture had a chef's contest called "A Taste of Colorado."

It was not your typical cowboy deal. It was adrift with suits, ties, and chic women. Waiters buzzed by offering libation.

As I reached for a Colorado Kool-Aid, one of the helpful program coordinators informed me that alcohol dulled the taste buds. Two hours earlier I had siphoned a gallon of gas from my pickup. If I had any buds left, they had lost their bloom.

Restauranteurs were displaying the best of their fare around the room. People walked by carrying little plates, gnawing on a teriyaki chicken wing, or popping fresh shrimp into their mouths.

"Did you try the blueberry eclair? Oh, that's right, you're a judge. You can't eat anything yet. Too bad, they're 'bout gone."

"Right." I smiled gamely, slobbering like a St. Bernard.

Just before I went into hypoglycemic shock, they announced the chefs were ready for the judges.

I won't attempt to repeat the names of the creations; suffice it to say they were not generic. I tried a bite of everything except the noodles. They reminded me of that advertisement for horse wormer.

I narrowed my choice to the Braised Piquant Lamb Graunier and the Roast Rolled Tenderloin Wilfamie à Rufus.

Our coach, a noted chef himself, stressed the importance of appearance and presentation. He drew our attention to the improperly trimmed artichoke stump. It looked like a cedar post someone had been at with a dull ax.

I noted it and focused on the white shavings next to the tenderloin. "Not enough contrast," said the coach. "Especially next to these yellowish things."

"Noodles," I reminded him.

Torn with indecision, I finally gave it to the lamb.

In the other categories, the winning appetizer was Trout Parfait and the winning salad looked like the flag of Honduras. The best dessert was apple pie, but they didn't call it that.

All of it was delicious, and I had a grand time despite the fact that the other judges disagreed with me about the winning entrée. As they said in Las Vegas when I hit the jackpot, "The turkey won."

Undaunted, I thanked them, cleansed my palate with Copenhagen, and bid them adieu.

Glossary

A chew: chewin' tobacco or snuff (Copenhagen).

Baler twine: has just about replaced balin' wire as the means of holdin' bales of hay together. However, this modernization has led to the deterioration of many small repair jobs on the farm for which only balin' wire would suffice. For instance, ya can't wire a loose exhaust pipe up to the frame with plastic twine.

Balling gun: a tube with a plunger about eighteen inches long used to administer large pills to livestock.

Bar ditch: slope-sided ditches along roads and highways.

Barrow: a castrated boar hog.

Blue heeler: a stock dog. Relies on a high pain threshold and bravado to move cattle. Bites at the heels. If the border collie is the quarterback, the blue heeler is the linebacker.

Border collie: a stock dog. Fairly universally acknowledged as the smartest of the species for the purpose intended. Favorite of North American and European sheepmen.

Brandin': a noun (as well as a verb) describing a big day in the spring when the calves (two to three months old) are roped and "drug to the fire" to be branded, ear marked, vaccinated, and castrated. It often involves hundreds of calves and lots of good help from the neighbors. It has social ramifications in the ranching community.

Braymer or Bramer: how you pronounce *Brahma,* a breed of cattle.

Buckin' stock: horses and bulls that perform in rodeo events: bareback bronc riding, saddle bronc riding, and bull riding.

Bulldoggin': a rodeo sport officially know as steer wrestling. A cowboy jumps off a galloping horse onto a galloping steer, catches it behind the horns, and with a twist and a flip throws it to the ground. It is a timed event and has no counterpart in the real cowboy world unless it's a bar fight.

Calculi: mineral formed in urine, which accumulates and often occludes the urethra—i.e., kidney stones.

Cod: usually refers to the testicleless fat-filled sack that remains after **a** bull is castrated.

Cow pucky: a pleasant euphemism for recycled grass and water.

D-8 Cats: bulldozers. D-8 is a model built by the Caterpillar company. It's a big'un.

Dehornin' blood: tiny but powerful arteries furnish cattle horns with blood. When cut they spray and leave a speckled pattern.

Doggers: the humans who compete in the rodeo event called steer wrestling (see also **Bulldoggin'**).

Faunching: pushing at or anticipating.

Feedlot: the less romantic side of the cowboy world. It is where steers (and heifers) spend their last three to four months eating grain before they become filet mignon.

Fence stay: a four-foot piece of twisted wire that keeps barbwire from saggin' between posts. You may also see stays made from Ocotillo skeletons, straight sticks, pieces of bedspring, or the occasional car axle.

Five buckle overshoes: standard footwear for cowboys in mud or snow. Fits over boots and rises to mid-calf (human). Thus, "five buckle deep" is a useful unit of measure.

Fleams: medieval surgical instruments used to "bleed a patient."

Floats: a metal instrument with a long handle and fitted with a small rasp on the business end. It is used to file the sharp points off equine molars. An ancient instrument still in regular use today. Also a verb . . . "How much do you charge to float teeth?"

Footrot: a disease of ungulates (cloven-hoofed beasts), otherwise self-explanatory.

Gelding: a castrated stallion.

Gummers: aged cows (ten years plus) who have lost their lower incisors. They do not have upper incisors (nor do sheep, goats, giraffes, yak—or my horseshoer, for that matter).

Gyp: a female dog.

Halter: fits over the head of horse or cow. It doesn't replace bridles or bits but it will hold an animal in place.

Heavy bunch: pregnant cows close to calving time.

Hog wire: or sheep wire, depending on yer part of the country. It is a woven fencing with vertical and horizontal wire crossing at eight-inch intervals like a tic-tac-toe board. Prevents smaller domestic farm animals from escaping. Will keep a dog outta the garden but not a coon or squirrel.

Horny toad: a species of desert reptile with spines.

Houlihan: a vertical loop used primarily to rope horses in a round corral.

Javelina: a peccary—a wild pig native to the Southwest. Tough little beasts, not very tasty.

Jiggin': an uncomfortable gait for the horse rider, akin to operating an airhammer or drivin' down a washboard dirt road.

Log chain: essential equipment around the farm. Used to pull dead stock or recalcitrant machinery, heavy feed troughs, or occasionally the wandering tourist vehicle from the ditch.

O.B. chains: obstetrical, chrome-plated chains, strong and lightweight, used in pulling calves. A loop is placed around each leg and gentle but firm traction is applied.

Polled: genetically hornless.

Prolapse: eversion, usually of the uterus, after calving. Replacing it has been compared to stuffing a thirty-pound rubber duck into a wine carafe.

Quakies: Aspen trees.

Quills: from porcupine quills. The forerunner of teat tubes, used to open, medicate, or partially drain a tight or diseased udder.

Ride (with) the wagon: in the old days (and on some outfits today) cowboys would go out to gather cattle for weeks at a time. The chuckwagon and bedwagon that accompanied them was home on the range at night.

Rollers in his nostrils: comparable to human flaring. The result of a sudden adrenaline rush. Usually accompanied by seein' the whites of their eyes.

Scour: (v) to have diarrhea. **Scours:** (n) as in "he's got the . . ."

Shoer: horseshoer—farrier, to be more exact.

Stock dog trials: competition among stock dogs and their trainers wherein cattle, sheep, or ducks are pushed through a circuitous course (go see the movie *Babe*).

Stock racks: high sides that fit in the back of a pickup (that's what those holes are for). Used to haul livestock.

Team roping: a rodeo event where the header ropes the steer's head and the heeler ropes the hind legs. Imitates real-life method of catching and restraining cattle on the open range.

Therio: short for the veterinary term *theriogenology,* the study of bovine (cow) reproduction.

Thirty-thirty: a good scabbard rifle.

Uterine boluses: a means of medicating the uterus postpartum. Usually applied with a plastic sleeve and a long arm.

Willers: common creek bank flora in the West. Can grow thick. A good place to hide or lay up in the shade. Not to be confused with weeping willows.

NPR Air Dates

1. Hangin' on, Hopin' and Prayin' for Rain
   Aired July of '88.
2. Ralph's Tree
   Aired August of '88.
3. All I Want for Christmas
   Aired Christmas, '88.
4. Runnin' Wild Horses
   Aired Spring of '89.
5. Anonymous End
   Aired Summer of '89.
6. Home the Hard Way
   Aired Fall of '89.
7. A Lesson in Life
   Aired December of '89.
8. The Sales Call
   Aired December of '89.
9. A Love Story
   Aired February of '90.
10. Holiday Travelers
    Aired February of '90.
11. The Car Wash
    Aired April of '90.
12. The Practitioner's Lot
    Aired Spring of '90.

13. AARP!
    Aired May of '90.

14. Range Fire
    Aired June of '90.

15. Chauvinist? Who Me?
    Aired June of '90.

16. Women!
    Aired August of '90.

17. Tolerance
    Aired September of '90.

18. Caught in the Act
    Aired September of '90.

19. Rudolph's Night Off
    Aired December of '90—repeated December of '91.

20. Grandma's Picture Box
    Aired December 12, '90.

21. Sheepmen, Border Collies, and Mules
    Aired January 8, '91.

22. The Consultant
    Aired February 13, '91.

23. Deer Rasslin'
    Aired February of '91.

24. Just Friends
    Aired April of '91.

25. Triggernometry
    Aired April of '91.

26. Oneupsmanship
    Aired May of '91.

27. The Ropin' Vet
    Aired June of '91

28. The Herd Sire
    Aired August 27, '91.

29. The Cowboy's Guide to Vegetarians
    Aired September of '91.

30. A Vegetarian's Guide to Cowboys
    Aired September of '91

31. The Stock Dog Demonstration
    Aired November 9, '91.

32. Cowboy Preserves
    Aired November 28, '91.

33. Fear of Flying
    Aired January 2, '92.

34. January, February, Mud
    Aired March 2, '92.

35. Boller's Comments
    Aired March 17, '92.

36. Another Good Man Gone
    Aired March 24, '92.

37. Lost
    Aired April 13, '92.

38. Ardel's Bull
    Aired May of '92.

39. Dog Emotions
    Aired May 28, '92.

40. 3% Markup
    Aired June 25, '92.

41. Secret Seasoning
    Aired July 7, '92.

42. Feast or Famine
    Aired July 23, '92—repeated June 4, '96

43. Loose Cow
    Aired August 5, '92.

44. Thrifty
    Aired November 10, '92.

45. Garthed Out!
    Aired November 16, '92.

46. Part Indian
    Aired November 25, '92.

47. White Oaks Rodeo
    Aired December 11, '92.

48. Joe and Maria
    Aired December 24, '92—repeated December of '94.

49. My Kinda Truck
    Aired January 13, '93.

50. Vern's Wreck
    Aired January 27, '93.

51. The Cowboy and His Tapeworm
    Aired February 3, '93.

52. Bentley the Born-Again Bull
    Aired February 12, '93.

53. Buffalo Tracks
    Aired February 26, '93.

54. The Great Chicken Run
    Aired March 5, '93.

55. Disappearing Digits
    Aired March 15, '93.

56. Lookin' Back
    Aired April 14, '93.

57. Political Correctness
    Aired May 1, '93.

58. The Big High and Lonesome
    Aired May of '93.

59. Landscaping
    Aired May of '93.

60. It Ain't Easy Bein' a Cowboy
    Aired June 3, '93.

61. The Old Stove-Up Cowboys of America
    Aired July of '93.

62. The Grapevine
    Aired July of '93.

63. The Tranquilizer Gun
    Aired August 4, '93.

64. Keepin' Busy
    Aired August 17, '93.

65. The Epitaph
    Aired August 20, '93.

66. A Fox in the Henhouse
    Aired September 2, '93.

67. Parakeets and Dogs
    Aired September 7, '93.

68. Cowboy Time
    Aired September 17, '93.

69. The Flood
   Aired September 22, '93.

70. Balin' Wheat
   Aired September 30, '93.

71. The Starr Valley Bean Field War
   Aired October 21, '93.

72. Chicago's Bratwurst
   Aired November 12, '93.

73. The National Insect
   Aired November 25, '93.

74. Moose Alert
   Aired December of '93.

75. What's Christmas to a Cow?
   Aired December 21, '93.

76. Cold Feet
   Aired January 31, '94.

77. Pig Tales
   Aired March 15, '94.

78. Tombstone of Canaan
   Aired April 4, '94.

79. Neat and Tidy Calving
   Aired April 13, '94.

80. The C-section
   Aired April 21, '94.

81. The Wilderness Wall
   Aired May 16, '94.

82. Advice Column
   Aired June 15, '94.

83. Border Collies
    Aired June 28, '94.

84. He Sang "Little Joe the Wrangler"
    Aired August 3, '94

85. The Outback
    Aired September 7, '94.

86. Truth in Labeling
    Aired September 26, '94.

87. It's the Law
    Aired October 6, '94.

88. The First Cowboy Thanksgiving
    Aired November 24, '94.

89. The Reindeer Flu
    Aired December 22, '94

90. Cowboy Mentality
    Aired January 12, '95.

91. The Valdez
    Aired February 8, '95.

92. The Mountain
    Aired February 14, '95.

93. Of Pigs and Poultry
    Aired March 1, '95.

94. Cow Xtractor
    Aired March 21, '95.

95. The Hunter's Son
    Aired March 27, '95.

96. Doggone Country
    Aired May 25, '95.

97. The Romantic Cowboy
    Aired June 5, '95.

98. A Cowboy Parade
    Aired June 23, '95.

99. Cow Attack
    Aired June 27, '95.

100. Anti-smokin' Device
    Aired August 15, '95.

101. High Cost of Recycling
    Aired August 28, '95.

102. In the Doghouse
    Aired September 22, '95.

103. Inheriting the Family Farm
    Aired September 27, '95.

104. The Lost Chicken
    Aired October 12, '95

105. Workin' for Wages
    Aired November 2, '95.

106. Minnesota Oreos
    Aired November 30, '95.

107. Oreos Apology
    Aired December 19, '95.

108. Leroy and Tom
    Aired January 2, '96.

109. Cowboy Vegetarian Cookbook
    Aired January 18, '96.

110. Noah's Dispersal Sale
    Aired February 12, '96.

111. Duct Tape in Agriculture
    Aired March 5, '96.
112. Cow Polygamy
    Aired April 12, '96.
113. Shoein' Pigeye
    Aired May 6, '96.
114. Nature Films
    Aired May 24, '96.
115. The Houlihan
116. Babe
    Aired September 9, '96.
117. Religious Reflections
    Aired October 10, '96.
118. Just Words
    Aired November 7, '96.
119 Here Come de Judge
    Aired November 13, '96.

FOR THE BEST IN PAPERBACKS, LOOK FOR THE 🐧

In every corner of the world, on every subject under the sun, Penguin represents quality and variety—the very best in publishing today.

For complete information about books available from Penguin—including Puffins, Penguin Classics, and Compass—and how to order them, write to us at the appropriate address below. Please note that for copyright reasons the selection of books varies from country to country.

In the United Kingdom: Please write to *Dept. EP, Penguin Books Ltd, Bath Road, Harmondsworth, West Drayton, Middlesex UB7 0DA.*

In the United States: Please write to *Penguin Putnam Inc., P.O. Box 12289 Dept. B, Newark, New Jersey 07101-5289* or call 1-800-788-6262.

In Canada: Please write to *Penguin Books Canada Ltd, 10 Alcorn Avenue, Suite 300, Toronto, Ontario M4V 3B2.*

In Australia: Please write to *Penguin Books Australia Ltd, P.O. Box 257, Ringwood, Victoria 3134.*

In New Zealand: Please write to *Penguin Books (NZ) Ltd, Private Bag 102902, North Shore Mail Centre, Auckland 10.*

In India: Please write to *Penguin Books India Pvt Ltd, 11 Panchsheel Shopping Centre, Panchsheel Park, New Delhi 110 017.*

In the Netherlands: Please write to *Penguin Books Netherlands bv, Postbus 3507, NL-1001 AH Amsterdam.*

In Germany: Please write to *Penguin Books Deutschland GmbH, Metzlerstrasse 26, 60594 Frankfurt am Main.*

In Spain: Please write to *Penguin Books S. A., Bravo Murillo 19, 1° B, 28015 Madrid.*

In Italy: Please write to *Penguin Italia s.r.l., Via Benedetto Croce 2, 20094 Corsico, Milano.*

In France: Please write to *Penguin France, Le Carré Wilson, 62 rue Benjamin Baillaud, 31500 Toulouse.*

In Japan: Please write to *Penguin Books Japan Ltd, Kaneko Building, 2-3-25 Koraku, Bunkyo-Ku, Tokyo 112.*

In South Africa: Please write to *Penguin Books South Africa (Pty) Ltd, Private Bag X14, Parkview, 2122 Johannesburg.*